SONGS OF THE COWBOYS

SONGS OF THE COWBOYS

Compiled by

N. HOWARD THORP

("Jack" Thorp)

Foreword by Guy Logsdon

University of Nebraska Press
Lincoln and London

First Bison Book printing: November 1984
   2   3   4   5   6   7   8   9   10

Library of Congress Cataloging in Publication Data
Main entry under title:
Songs of the cowboys.
  Reprint. Originally published: Boston : Houghton
Mifflin, c1921.
   1. Cowboys — Poetry. 2. Cowboys — Songs and music —
Texts. 3. West (U.S.) — Poetry. 4. American poetry — West
(U.S.) 5. Ballads, English — West (U.S.) — Texts.
I. Thorp, N. Howard (Nathan Howard), 1867–1940.
PS595.C6S6 1984   784.4'978   84-11872
ISBN 0-8032-4410-X
ISBN 0-8032-9403-4 (pbk.)

∞

ACKNOWLEDGMENTS

I wish to acknowledge the use of songs from the following authors: James Barton Adams, Charles Badger Clark, Larry Chittenden, Alice Corbin, Austin Corcoran, J. W. Foley, Henry Herbert Knibbs, Phil Le Noir.

"A Cowboy's Prayer"; "A Border Affair," and "High-Chin Bob" are published by permission of Richard G. Badger from *Sun and Saddle Leather*, by Badger Clark; "Sky-High"; "Old Hank"; "The Little Cow-girl"; "Pecos Tom"; "'Light, Stranger, 'Light"; "Women Outlaws"; "Old Paint," and "What's Become of the Punchers?" by N. Howard Thorp, were published in *Poetry: A Magazine of Verse,* in August, 1920; and Phil LeNoir's "Ol' Dynamite" and "Down on the Ol' Bar-G" in the same number of the magazine. The cowboy version of "High-Chin Bob," by Charles Badger Clark, was published in *Poetry* in August, 1917. Henry Herbert Knibbs's "Punchin' Dough" appeared in the *Popular Magazine.*

Phil LeNoir is the author of *Rhymes of the Wild and Woolly* (Phil LeNoir, Las Vegas, N.M.); Charles Badger Clark, of *Sun and Saddle Leather* and *Grass Grown Trails* (Richard G. Badger, Boston); Henry Herbert Knibbs, of *Songs of the Outlands, Riders of the Stars* and *Songs of the Trail* (Houghton Mifflin Company, Boston).

Larry Chittenden, author of "The Cowboys' Christmas Ball" in this volume, has a book of songs called *Ranch Verses* (G. P. Putnam's Sons, New York).

N. H. T.

CONTENTS

Foreword
By Guy Logsdon

When the cowboy galloped romantically out of the Southwest, his folk life—or at least the *myth* of it—was branded deeply into the culture of the United States and other countries as well. Through newspapers, magazines, literature, motion pictures, television, and particularly through songs, the romanticized cowboy has been received either voluntarily or involuntarily into the homes of virtually every citizen of this nation. Our language, clothing, foods, and music reflect the impact of the romanticized cowboy, but through the decades since that first range herd was driven out of Texas northward into a myth of the Southwest, there have remained a large number of working cowboys who have maintained the authentic cowboy folk culture. Such a real cowboy was Jack Thorp.

Nathan Howard "Jack" Thorp was an unusual man. He was a cultured New Yorker who became a genuine cowboy. He was the first to collect, systematically with a purpose, songs sung by cowboys and the first to publish a collection of them. He was a poet who lived long enough to see one of his compositions become universally accepted as a favorite traditional cowboy song. And he was a collector and teller of stories—particularly horse stories—of which many were committed to print. Jack Thorp was, indeed, a cattleman, horseman, rancher, poet, and storyteller.

Little is known about Thorp's life, even though his autobiography, *Pardner of the Wind,* was published in 1945 and reprinted by the University of Nebraska Press (BB 638) in 1977. Neil M. Clark collaborated as editor and ghost writer with Thorp in preparing the manuscript before Thorp's death in 1940. Clark's introduction contained only a short statement about Thorp's early life; the bulk of the autobiography reflected Thorp's range experiences and told his stories. (In an interview on December 31, 1979, in his Santa Fe home, Clark at the age of eighty-nine could recall only that Thorp was a large man; therefore, his introduction remains the primary biographical source.)

The year—1867—that Joseph McCoy opened Abilene, Kansas, to trail herders and Texas cattle was the year of Thorp's birth in New York City on June 10. His father was a prominent lawyer who provided his children with cultural and educational opportunities; Thorp was educated at Saint Paul's School in Concord, New Hampshire. However, due to unwise real estate investments his father's financial structure collapsed, so Jack (how he acquired the nickname is not known) was unable to attend college. Since he had been spending his summers on his brother's ranch near Stanton, Nebraska, he stayed there after his father's financial reverses. He moved to New Mexico in 1886.

There, at the age of nineteen, Jack applied cowboy skills that he had learned in Nebraska and turned to cowboying for life. While learning more about that work, he engaged successfully in buying and trading horses that could be shipped to New York to be trained as polo ponies. In New York, Thorp had learned to ride horses as a polo player; for a few years his horse trading made enough money for him to return there each year during the polo season.

During Thorp's second year in New Mexico, while he hunted for stray horses, his life took a new turn, as recounted in "Banjo in the Cow Camps," the first chapter of *Pardner of the Wind*.[1] On a March night in 1889, Thorp crossed the Pecos River above Roswell, New Mexico, and rode into the night camp of Nigger Add, the range boss of the L F S Ranch. As he rode toward the camp, he heard a cowboy singing about "the fastest cutting-horse in Texas," Dodgin' Joe (the song, lost from cowboy lore, has never appeared in any collection). After supper, he inquired about "Dodgin' Joe" and asked for more songs. What he heard inspired him to continue traveling, not to hunt for horses but for songs, armed with his mandolin-banjo and a notebook. His decision was sudden, impulsive. At the age of twenty-one, he saw the tracking down of songs as an adventure. The next morning Thorp set out on a collecting trip that lasted one year and covered fifteen hundred miles; that took him into Texas, Indian

Territory, and back to New Mexico; and that made him the first field collector of cowboy songs.

"Banjo in the Cow Camps" contains the most accurate reflections about cowboy songs and singing that have been published:

In the nineties, with the exception of about a dozen, cowboy songs were not generally known. The only ones I could find I gathered, a verse here and a verse there. . . . (P. 22)

That was one of the difficulties encountered in the earliest effort to assemble the unprinted verse of the range. None of the cowboys who could sing ever remembered an entire song. (P. 23)

Cowboy songs were always sung by one person, never by a group. I never did hear a cowboy with a real good voice; if he had one to start with, he always lost it bawling at cattle, or sleeping out in the open, or tellin' the judge he didn't steal that horse. (P. 27)

The cowboy hardly ever knew what tune he was singing his song to; just some old, old tune that he had heard and known as a boy. (P. 27)

It is generally thought that cowboys did a lot of singing around the herd at night to quiet them on the bed ground. I have been asked about this, and I'll say that I have stood my share of night watches in fifty years, and I seldom heard any singing of that kind. (P. 29)

Thorp, in concise statements supported with stories, said more about real cowboy songs and singing than all of the romanicizers who have followed. Finally, like later collectors and chroniclers, he noted that many cowboy songs were obscene.

Cowboy songs, as I have said, were full of the vernacular of the range, and it wasn't always parlor talk. I vividly remember . . . the entire range version of "The Top Hand"! The theme—ridicule of a cowboy too big for his boots—was a scorcher in itself, and the words of the song would have burned the reader's eyeballs if printed as Jim sang it. (P. 41)

Thorp expurgated it (probably, he bowdlerized it, but he may have removed some verses). He included it in his first book of cowboy songs, and in subsequent collections "The Top Hand" appeared exactly as he printed it in 1908.

Thorp returned to his home range in New Mexico in March 1889 and went back to work for the outfit that he had ridden away from the year before. The years immediately following are hazy, for only generalizations and often undated stories compose the rest of his autobiography. A few writers have quoted Thorp's account of being in the first Oklahoma land run on April 22, 1889, but apparently they failed to read the introduction to Chapter Three, in which he wrote: "Although I did not make that drive myself, I have written the story of it as if I were along; as I might have been, since I was a Bar W hand and knew all the boys who went" (p. 89). Thorp based the account on stories that he had heard; his use of the first person pronouns *I* and *we* makes it sound convincingly autobiographical, when in fact, he was simply a great storyteller.

J. Frank Dobie attested to Thorp's narrative skill in *The Long-horns* (1941) by using some of Thorp's stories and by dedicating Chapter Five, "Stompedes," to him. On February 11, 1941, Dobie wrote about Thorp to Neil Clark: "He sent me a story about an old timer getting down in a pit and fighting a grizzly bear. That is as good a bear story as I ever read. About a little over a year ago I used it in a Sunday newspaper feature, paying him for it and sending him my revision of his story."

An even more revealing description of Thorp was given by Dobie in the same letter:

I never was with Jack Thorp as much as I wish I had been with him. I went out to his little place at Alameda one afternoon, having left Albuquerque with the intention of getting to Santa Fe that night. When the sun was about down I said I had to go, but Jack said no I had better wait. I waited and we had supper and then kept on talking until away after midnight. I did manage to get to Santa Fe the next afternoon. All Jack needed was a good listener. He never seemed to run out and yet his stories always had pertinence and were based on character more than on anything else. He had a wonderful memory. His sense of humor, his sweetness of nature and his adequate use of observation made his memory a useful and delightful agent.[2]

Dobie used, without identifying his source, Thorp material in *Apache Gold and Yaqui Silver* (1939), but in *The Mustangs* (1952) he gave praise and credit before telling one of Thorp's stories. And in *Some Part of Myself* (1967) Dobie noted in his chapter "Story-tellers I Have Known" the same visit that was described in his letter to Clark. Not only Dobie admired Thorp but also two other bookmen and bibliographers, Jeff Dykes and Ramon Adams, who have written praises about his authenticity as a southwestern cowboy and story-teller. Therefore, it is not known how many of the events he described in the first person were entirely correct or how much embellishment was added to create a good story.

Nevertheless, according to Clark, Thorp had received training as a civil engineer and worked, probably during the early 1890s, for the Enterprise Mining Company at Kingston, New Mexico. Following this work, he returned to or resumed a full-time life in cattle and horse ranching in New Mexico and continued to collect songs. And he became a cowboy poet whose poems were accepted by other cowboys.

If Thorp had written only "Little Joe, the Wrangler," he still would stand out as a great cowboy poet, for "Little Joe" remains one of the most popular cowboy songs in oral tradition. His storytelling ability found poetic form when one night in 1898, while helping trail-herd cattle from Chimney Lake, New Mexico, to Higgins, Texas, he wrote on a paper bag the tragic story of Little Joe. Using the popular tune of "The Little Old Log Cabin in the Lane," he sang it to the men on the drive. (In his 1921 edition of *Songs of the Cowboys* he identified the other cowboys). On the return trip he sang it in "Uncle Johnny Root's store and saloon at Weed, New Mexico"; it quickly spread through the Southwest, and many cowboys claimed to have known and worked with Little Joe. Today it is not unusual to hear a cowboy say that either his dad or granddad knew Little Joe. But his real identity died with Thorp.

When the recording industry in the 1920s turned to cowboy singers as a new source of talent and market, "Little Joe" was one of the early releases; in 1940 Thorp asserted that 375,000 records of it had been sold, but he had never received a penny of royalty as its author. Earlier, in 1932, he hired the law firm of Botts and Botts in Albuquerque to file a lawsuit for royalty payments; after three years of seeking advice and assistance from other law firms in New York and Washington, D.C., Botts and Botts with Thorp's approval dropped the suit, giving the opinion that composers of popular songs did not always receive royalties and that five years had lapsed between the first release of the recording and the filing of the lawsuit. By the 1930s Thorp could have used the money that royalties would have provided.

On December 22, 1903, Thorp and Annette Hesch, the daughter of a sheepman, were married in Palma, New Mexico; it was a childless but happy marriage that lasted until his death. The Thorps maintained the cattle-ranching life; from 1913 to 1918 he was cattle inspector for the state of New Mexico. But prior to this, he became a publisher.

Thorp had been writing in a notebook his own poems and songs, along with those that he collected, and he began to visualize them as a book. When he eventually settled a few miles north of Albuquerque, near Alameda, he turned to a printer, P. A. Speckman, who operated the News Print Shop in nearby Estancia. In 1908 Thorp paid Speckman six cents per copy to print two thousand copies of twenty-three songs (fifty pages) under the title *Songs of the Cowboys*—a few cents per copy for a book that now commands thousands of dollars in the rare books market. It was the first published collection of cowboy songs, but no music or melody lines were included, only the texts, and among the titles were at least five songs written by Thorp—"Little Joe, the Wrangler," "Chopo," "The Pecos River Queen," "Whose Old Cow," and "Speckles"—along with his version of "Top Hand." He sold the books through newspaper ads for fifty cents each and gave many to friends.[3]

Two years later, in 1910, John A. Lomax published his *Cowboy Songs and Other Frontier Ballads,* which received international distribution and quickly became the standard cowboy songbook. It influenced cowboy singers even into the present era by standardizing texts. But, even though Lomax created the impression that all of the songs were collected in the field, evidence now proves that many of the songs in his book were acquired through correspondence with singers and other collectors. It is not known definitely that he had a copy of Thorp's publication, but he did include nineteen selections from *Songs of the Cowboys,* most of which varied little from Thorp's text. "The Top Hand" was included exactly as Thorp had rewritten it. The problem was that Lomax did not give credit to his sources.[4] In 1916 a new, enlarged edition of the Lomax collection was issued, again with no source citations. Thorp was angered about the omission, but Lomax could not have known that he wrote "Little Joe." However, he could have credited Thorp's *Songs of the Cowboys.*

Thorp continued to write poems and songs, with a few being published in newspapers and livestock journals, and he continued to collect songs, which were more abundant because of the increased number of cowboy poets and the Lomax books. Also, the eastern intellectual and art circles were becoming infatuated with the *romantic* Indians and cowboys of New Mexico, so there was a growing audience for cowboy poems and songs. In the August 1920 issue of *Poetry,* Harriet Monroe printed eight of Thorp's poems, along with some "western" ones by Phil LeNoir. Their inclusion in *Poetry* was justified in an essay about folk poetry by Alice Corbin Henderson. Two of Thorp's poems were reprinted in the August 21, 1920, issue of the *Literary Digest.* Apparently this prestigious recognition, along with the challenge by Lomax and a growing national market for cowboy lore, inspired Thorp to expand his first published collection.

Thorp had a copy of the 1916 edition of Lomax's book; with ironic humor he used it in preparing his new edition. When applicable, he wrote such notes as "my own, taken from my book" or "as expunged by me." For those sixty-nine songs not in his own book but which he knew, Thorp wrote "Have," and many of them he used in his new collection. Because he made many textual corrections and changes, the songs were not always identical to those in the Lomax text. However, one song that Thorp had collected in fragments during his 1889 trip was "Sam Bass"; he had pieced together a nine-verse narrative for use in 1908, and Lomax had published eleven verses that had a smoother flow of words and rhythm. Thorp used the Lomax text, changing only a few punctuation marks. He reversed their roles by giving Lomax no credit.

Thorp used all but one of the songs that were in his 1908 book. Why he chose to exclude "The Cowboys' New Year's Dance" is not

known, but it was never a traditional song and its author is unknown. It has appeared in only one other collection, *The Happy
Cowboy Sings and Plays Songs of Pioneer Days,* edited by Kenneth S.
Clark and published by Paull-Pioneer Music Corporation in 1934.
Clark credited Thorp as the author and set it to music; since Clark
corresponded with cowboy poets and collectors as he prepared his
manuscript, he probably got his information from Thorp. If so, it
increases the number of original songs in Thorp's 1908 edition.
Thorp's expanded collection was published in 1921 by Houghton
Mifflin Company under the original title, *Songs of the Cowboys;* 101
songs were included along with an introduction by Alice Corbin
Henderson. Although her definition of folk song was broader than
scholars would accept, she wrote an interesting essay that contained
one important concept for collectors: "it is the *use* of a song, rather
than its origin, which determines what is known as folk-song." Also,
Henderson considered the efforts of cowboy poets in the context of
literary criticism; she did not separate the idea of collecting pieces
from oral tradition from individual authorship in printed form; to
Henderson it was folk poetry (song) if the folk idiom was a device of
style. In fact, her interpretations are more pertinent to literary than
to oral tradition, which was and is important for this particular
collection. The 1921 edition of *Songs of the Cowboys* should have
been entitled "Songs and Poems," for Thorp included many poems
from non-oral tradition, and no music or melody lines were printed.
  Of the 101 songs or poems, 27 were written by Thorp, most of
which never entered oral tradition. Regarding the other songs, he
identified the author when possible, and he acknowledged where,
when, and from whom (except Lomax) he collected the songs.
Although he did not acknowledge Lomax, later, in *Pardner of the
Wind,* he referred to him as "a learned professor." His notes were
concise, except when the opportunity for humor arose. For "Old-
Time Cowboy" (p. 121), he noted: "written by an old cow-puncher
who claims he was dragging his rope along and someone else's calf
got tangled up in it." Thirty of the songs were definitely from or still
in oral tradition. Another thirty had apparently been lost from oral
tradition, for he had heard them sung but they had not been collected by anyone else. Forty-one were poems with the author iden-

tified for most of them. Indeed, Thorp compiled a unique collection with the emphasis on text, not music; he saved many cowboy songs and poems from probable extinction.

Thorp continued to collect and write, and he privately published a collection of stories, *Tales of the Chuck Wagon,* in 1926; it did not get widespread distribution or recognition. But like his songs, the tales were those he had heard at night in the cowcamps; they captured the real cowboy in spirit, humor, and language. Also, Thorp continued to publish poems and stories in newspapers and journals around his home territory, but at no time did he receive national recognition as *the* pioneer collector and cowboy poet that he deserved.

As cattlemen and cowboys know, most of the old-timers did not accumulate great wealth; Jack and Annette Thorp were no exceptions. In the 1930s they lived a modest life two miles north of Alameda, while his health—but not his spirit—waned; during those years he worked on a novel that was not published and has since been lost. The evening of June 4, 1940, while sitting in a chair and talking with his wife in their home, Jack Thorp died. A sizable piece of southwestern lore died with him, but he left a legacy of songs, poems, and stories (often used by others as their own) that have enriched the heritage of the real cowboy.

Notes

1. A slightly modified version with the same title was published in the August 1940 issue of *Atlantic Monthly.*

2. J. Frank Dobie, *The Longhorns* (Boston: Little, Brown and Company, 1941), p. 6.

3. For an in-depth study of Thorp's first book, see Jack Thorp, *Songs of the Cowboys,* ed. Austin E. and Alta S. Fife (New York: Clarkson N. Potter, Inc., 1966).

4. For a study of the Lomax-Thorp controversy, see D. K. Wilgus, *Anglo-American Folksong Scholarship Since 1898* (New Brunswick, N. J.: Rutgers University Press, 1959), and John O. West, "Jack Thorp and John Lomax: Oral or Written Transmission?" *Western Folklore* 26 (April 1967), 113–18.

SONGS OF THE COWBOYS

THE ARIZONA BOYS AND GIRLS

Don't know the author. Heard it sung by Kitt Collins in Deming, New Mexico.

Come, all of you people, I pray you draw near,
A comical ditty I promise you'll hear.
The boys in this country they try to advance
By courting the ladies and learning to dance.

The boys in this country they try to be plain —
Those words that you hear you may hear them
         again
With twice as much added on if you can.
There's many a boy who thinks he's a man.

They'll go to their parties, their whiskey they'll
         take,
And out in the dark their bottles they'll break;
You'll hear one say, "There's a bottle round here;
So come around, boys, and we'll all take a share."

There is some wears shoes and some wears boots,
But there are very few that rides who don't shoot;
More than this I'll tell you what they'll do,
They'll get them a watch and a ranger hat too;

They'll go in the hall with spurs on their heel;
They'll get them a partner to dance the next reel,

Saying, "How do I look in my new brown suit,
With my pants stuffed down in the top of my boot?"

Now, I think it's quite time to leave off these
      lads,
For here are some girls that's fully as bad;
They'll trim up their dresses and curl up their
      hair,
And like an old owl 'fore the looking-glass stare.

The girls in the country they grin like a cat,
And with giggling and laughing don't know where
        they're at;
They think they're pretty, and I tell you they're
        wise,
But they could n't get married to save their two eyes.

You can tell a good girl wherever she's found;
No trimming, no laces, no nonsense around;
With a long-eared bonnet tied under her chin, —
She'll marry you if you are broke or if you have the
        tin.

They'll go to church with their snuff-box in hand,
They'll give it a tap to make it look grand;
Perhaps there is another one or two
And they'll pass it around and it's "Madam, won't
        you?"

Now, I think it's quite time for this ditty to end;
If there's any one here that it will offend,
If there's any one here that thinks it amiss,
Just come round and give the singer a kiss.

ARROYO AL'S COW-PONY

By J. A. Squires, Helena, Montana

I first heard this sung in a cow-camp in Guadalupe Mountains, New Mexico.

I took a trip this summer to the market,
And I struck an Eastern city where they sell you
    tubs of beers;
I was feelin' pretty yowlish and I could n't say my
    name,
When I wound up somehow 'nuther at a high-toned
    polo game.

There were sunburned doods cavortin' on some
    ponies in a lot,
And they whacked a little ball till it traveled like a
    shot;
I could n't savvy, nohow, and I vowed that I was
    through,
When I spied a feller ridin' on a pony that I knew.

It was that there buckskin bronco that I rode for
    the Circle Bar;
He was clipped and oiled and powdered, but I knew
    each old-time scar;
I had lost him when Bear Hawkins played an extra
    ace and jack,
And I'd allus had a longin' fer to git that pony back.

Well, he sorter stopped and snorted when I give
    an old-time "Yip!"
And he bucked until his rider hit the ground upon
    his hip;

And he came a-runnin' to me and I jumped upon
   his back,
And he pitched for sheer enjoyment when I hit his
   flank a whack.

Well, I rode across the open and I stooped down o1
   the run,
And picked up the polo mallet (fer the player he
   was done),
And I hit that ball a crack, sir, and it sailed plum
   o'er the fence,
And the crowd just howled with pleasure, fer they
   thought the sport immense.

Well, it cost me just six hundred fer to git my little
   bronk,
And to have that player patched up from his heels to
   injured conk;
But I got my old cow-pony — and jest hear this one
   thing more:
Don't whisper "polo" to him or he'll buck like
   Satan, shore!

THE BIBLICAL COWBOY

Sent me by Jim Hagan, of Tulsa, Oklahoma

All day long on the prairies I ride,
Not even a dog to trot by my side;
My fire I kindle with chips gathered round,
My coffee I boil without being ground.

I wash in a pool and wipe on a sack;
I carry my wardrobe all on my back;

For want of an oven I cook bread in a pot,
And sleep on the ground for want of a cot.

My ceiling the sky, my floor is the grass,
My music is the lowing herds as they pass;
My books are the brooks, my sermons the stones;
My parson the wolf on his pulpit of bones.

And then, if cooking is not complete,
You can't blame me for wanting to eat.
But show me a man that sleeps more profound
Than the big puncher-boy stretching out on the
    ground.

My books teach me ever consistence to prize,
My sermons that small things I should not despise;
My parson remarks from his pulpit of bones
That fortune favors those who look out for their own.

And then between me and love lies a gulf wide:
Some lucky fellow may call her his bride.
My friends gently hint I am coming to grief,
But men must make money and women have beef.

But Cupid is always a friend to the bold,
And the best of his arrows are pointed with gold.
As society bans me, so savage I dodge,
And the Masons would ball me out of their lodge.

If I had hair on my chin I might pass for the goat
That bore all the sins in the ages remote;
But why it is I cannot understand,
That each of the patriarchs owned a big brand.

Abraham emigrated in search of a range,
And when water was scarce he wanted a change;
Old Isaac owned cattle in charge of Esau,
And Jacob punched cows for his father-in-law.

He started in business way down at bed rock,
And made quite a stake at handling stock;
Then David went from night-herding to using a
    sling;
And winning the battle he became a great king;
Then the shepherds, while herding the sheep on a
    hill,
Got a message from heaven of peace and good
    will.

BILLY THE KID
or
WILLIAM H. BONNEY
By N. Howard Thorp

*Down in Lincoln the native women still scare their chil-
dren with the threat that Bilito will come and get them if
they don't behave.*

Bustin' down the canyon,
Horses on the run,
Posse just behind them,
'T was June first, seventy-one.

Saddle guns in scabbards,
Pistols on saddle bow,
The boys were ridin' for their lives —
The Kid en Alias Joe.

Thirty miles west of the Gila
They bade the posse good-bye,
For they could n't keep up with the light-
    weight Kids,
Now matter how hard they'd try.

From the land of the Montezuma,
Past the hills of the Mogollons,
By night en day they made their way
Till they landed in Tombstone.

Those were frontier towns, old pardner;
'T was a game of take en give,
And the one who could draw the fastest
Was the only one who'd live.

Whiskey en women en poker,
Monte en Faro en Stud,
Just a short wild race, who'd keep the pace
Would land in a river of blood.

Fightin' en drinkin' en gamblin',
Nigger en Mex en White;
'T was a riot of sin, let the best man win;
'T was drink, when called, or fight.

En every one claimed a woman,
Though none of their claims would stand
'Gainst the Kid, who was quicker'n lightning
With a gun in either hand.

Believing that John H. Tunstall
Was the man who was in the right,

He offered him his services
In the Lincoln County fight.

The Kid rode with Brewer's posse
Who avenged John Tunstall's loss,
Killing William Morton, en Baker
Roberts en Joe Ross.

Locked in the Dolan house in Lincoln,
Then used as a county jail,
Handcuffed en with a double guard,
Trailing a ball en chain,

He killed his guards, Bell en Olinger,
In the jail yard in daylight,
Stole the horse of the probate clerk
En on him made his flight.

Caught a-napping at last in Sumner,
In Pete Maxwell's room one night,
Not knowing he was waylaid,
Not knowing with whom to fight;

A chance shot fired by Garrett,
A chance shot that found its mark;
'T was lucky for Pat the Kid showed plain,
While Garrett was hid in the dark.

If Garrett was game, I don't know it;
He never appeared so to me;
If any of you fellows think so,
I'll refer you to Oliver Lee.

*P.S. Oliver, if you happen to see this, don't shoot through
the water-tank and drown me.*   *Jack*

THE BOOZER

Cut this out of a Colorado newspaper

I'm a howler from the prairies of the West!
If you want to die with terror look at me!
I'm chain-lightning — if I ain't, may I be blessed!
I'm the snorter of the boundless prairie!

He's a killer and a hater!
He's the great annihilator!
He's a terror of the boundless prairie!

I'm the snoozer from the upper trail!
I'm the reveler in murder and in gore!
I can bust more Pullman coaches on the rail
Than any one who's worked the job before.

He's a snorter and a snoozer!
He's the great trunk line abuser!
He's the man who puts the sleeper on the rail!

I'm the double-jawed hyena from the East!
I'm the blazing bloody blizzard of the States!
I'm the celebrated slugger; I'm the Beast!
I can snatch a man bald-headed while he waits!

He's a double-jawed hyena!
He's the villain of the scena!
He can snatch a man bald-headed while he waits!

A BORDER AFFAIR

By Charles Badger Clark, Jr.

Sung by Orville Cox, a Taos Cowboy

Spanish is the lovin' tongue,
Soft as music, light as spray:
'T was a girl I learnt it from,
Livin' down Sonora way.
I don't look much like a lover,
Yet I say her love words over
Often when I'm all alone —
" Mi amor, mi corazon."

Nights when she knew where I'd ride
She would listen for my spurs,
Fling the big door open wide,
Raise them laughin' eyes of hers,
And my heart would nigh stop beatin'
When I heard her tender greetin',
Whispered soft for me alone —
" Mi amor, mi corazon! "

Moonlight in the patio,
Old Señora noddin' near,
Me and Juana talkin' low
So the Madre could n't hear —
How those hours would go a-flyin'!
And too soon I'd hear her sighin'
In her little sorry tone —
" Adios, mi corazon! "

But one time I had to fly
For a foolish gamblin' fight,

And we said a swift good-bye
In that black unlucky night.
When I'd loosed her arms from clingin'
With her words the hoofs kept ringin'
As I galloped north alone —
"Adios, mi corazon!"

Never seen her since that night —
I kaint cross the Line, you know.
She was Mex, and I was white;
Like as not it's better so.
Yet I've always sort of missed her
Since that last wild night I kissed her;
Left her heart and lost my own —
"Adios, mi corazon!"

BRONC PEELER'S SONG

*Authorship unknown. First heard sung by L. Brennon,
at Indian Tanks, New Mexico.*

I've been upon the prairie,
I've been upon the plain,
I've never rid a steamboat,
Nor a double-cinched-up train.
But I've driv my eight-up to wagon
That were locked three in a row,
And that through blindin' sand-storms,
And all kinds of wind and snow.

There never was a place I've been
Had any kind of wood:
We burn the roots of bar-grass
And think it's very good.

I've never tasted home bread,
Nor cakes nor muss like that;
But I know fried dough and beef
Pulled from red-hot tallow fat.

I hate to see the wire fence
A-closin' up the range;
And all this fillin' in the trail
With people that is strange.
We fellers don't know how to plough,
Nor reap the golden grain;
But to round up steers and brand the cows
To us was allus plain.

So when this blasted country
Is all closed in with wire,
And all the top as trot grass
Is burnin' in Sol's fire,
I hope the settlers will be glad
When rain hits the land,
And all us cowdogs are in hell
With a "set" joined hand in hand.

BRONCO JACK'S THANKSGIVING

By James Barton Adams

Heard this recited by a young lady at a Cowboys' Reunion at Las Vegas, New Mexico, and afterwards learned the author's name.

'T was this time jest a year ago on this Thanks-
       givin' Day,
That me an' Bronco Jack stood up, an' pa gave me
       away.

An' Parson Billy spoke the words that made us
    man and wife,
To run as double-header team along the trail of life.
We had a combination feast, half weddin' dinner an'
The other half Thanksgivin' an' I tell you it was
    grand;
An' everybody that was there allowed the dance
    jest tuk
The cake from any ranch event that they had ever
    struck.

They all kep' sayin' Jack was wild, an' some allowed
    that he
Was hardly fit to share the life o' sich gal as me.
But I was of a reckless turn, an' tol' 'em that I hoped
To have success in tamin' him when I had got him
    roped.
There's quite a change of feelin' now, fer ever sence
    the day,
We j'ined our hands an' tuk the vows to make a
    double play,
He's proved as good a husban' as a woman ever got,
An' all the gals is jealous of the thorrerbred I
    caught.

The only thing that's rattled him was when the
    Master sent
Two great big bouncin' baby twins to us: the said
    event
Jest seemin' fer to break him up, him sayin', sort
    o' gruff,
That one sich infant music-box he thought was
    quite enough;

But now he's sort o' reconciled: I of'n hear him
    talk
About 'em bein' pedigreed an' fancy blooded stock;
An' though he yit holds to it that I played it rather
    bold,
I know he would n't part with one fer twice its
    weight in gold.

As we was settin' here last night a-talkin' 'bout the
    day,
An' all that we was thankful fer, I said, in a jokin'
    way:
"Now, tell me, honest Injun, Jack, dead earnest
    an' fer fair,
If you ain't filled with gratitude a-lookin' at that
    pair?"
He gazed down at the sleepin' kids a-layin' side by
    side,
With what I sort o' 'magined was a look o' daddy
    pride.
An' said: "They're fine as silk an' I ain't makin'
    any roar,
But I am mighty thankful that there was n't any
    more!"

BUCKING BRONCO

By Belle Star, Indian Territory

*Written about 1878. Song has been expurgated by me.
The author was a member of a notorious gang of outlaws, but a very big-hearted woman. I knew her well.*

My love is a rider, wild broncos he breaks,
Though he's promised to quit it, just for my sake

He ties up one foot, the saddle puts on,
With a swing and a jump he is mounted and gone.

The first time I met him, 't was early one spring,
Riding a bronco, a high-headed thing.
He tipped me a wink as he gayly did go,
For he wished me to look at his bucking bronco.

The next time I saw him, 't was late in the fall,
Swinging the girls at Tomlinson's ball:
He laughed and he talked as we danced to and
   fro, —
Promised never to ride on another bronco.

He made me some presents, among them a ring;
The return that I made him was a far better thing;
'T was a young maiden's heart, I'd have you all
   know
He'd won it by riding his bucking bronco.

Now, all you young maidens, where'er you reside,
Beware of the cowboy who swings the rawhide,
He'll court you and pet you and leave you and go
In the spring up the trail on his bucking bronco.

BUCKSKIN JOE

Author unknown. First heard this recited by a medicine-vendor in Waco, Texas, on the public square.

'T was a calm and peaceful evening in a camp called
   Arapahoe,
And the whiskey was a-running with a soft and
   gentle flow;

The music was a-ringing in a dance-hall 'cross the
way,
And the dancers was a-swinging just as close as
they could lay.

People gathered round the tables a-betting of
their wealth,
And near by stood a stranger who had come there
for his health.
He was a peaceful stranger, though he seemed to
be unstrung;
For just before he'd left his home he'd been sep-
arated from one lung.

Near by at a table sat a man named Hankey Dean,
A tougher man than Hankey leather chaps had
never seen.
But Hankey was a gambler and he sure did hate
to lose;
And he had just parted with a sun-dried stack of
blues.

He arose from the table, on the floor his last chip
flung,
And cast his fiery glimmers on the man with just
one lung.
"No wonder I've been losing every bet I made to-
night
When a sucker and a tenderfoot was 'tween me
and the light.

"Look here, little stranger, do you know who I am?"
"Yes, and I don't care a copper-colored damn."

The dealers stopped their dealing and the players
    held their breath;
For words like those to Hankey were a sudden flirt
    with death.

"Listen, gentle stranger, I'll read my pedigree:
I'm known for handling tenderfeet and worser
    men than thee;
The lions on the mountains I've drove them to
    their lairs;
The wild-cats are my playmates and I've wrestled
    grizzly bears;

"Why, the centipedes can't sorter mar my tough old
    hide,
And rattlesnakes have bit me and crawled off and
    died.
I'm as wild as the wildest horse that ever roamed
    the range;
The moss grows on my teeth and wild blood flows
    through my veins.

"I'm wild and woolly and full of fleas,
And never curried below the knees.
Now, little stranger, if you'll give me your address —
How would you like to go, by fast mail or express?"

The little stranger, who was leaning against the door,
Picked up a hand of playing cards that were scat-
    tered on the floor.
Picking out the five o' spades, he pinned it to the door,
And then stepped backward some twenty steps or
    more.

He pulled out his life-preserver and with a "one,
    two, three, four,"
Blotted out a spot with every pistol roar;
For he had traveled with a circus, and had only quit
    that day.
"I have one more left, kind sir, if you wish to call
    the play."

Then Hank stepped up to the stranger, and this is
    the way he spoke:
"Why, the lions in the mountains — that was
    nothing but a joke;
Never mind about the extra — you are a bad shoot-
    ing man,
And I'm a meek child and as harmless as a lamb."

CALIFORNIA TRAIL

By Kate Childs ("Montana Kate")

*Written about 1869. I heard it sung first on Pecos River,
at Horse Head Crossing, in 1900, by Sam Murray.*

List, all you California boys,
And open wide your ears,
For now we start across the plains
With a herd of mules and steers.
Now bear in mind, before you start,
That you'll eat jerked beef, not ham,
And antelope steak, oh, cuss the stuff!
It often proves a sham.

You cannot find a stick of wood
On all this prairie wide;
Whene'er you eat you've got to stand
Or sit on some old bull-hide.

It's fun to cook with buffalo chips
Or mesquite green as corn, —
If I'd once known what I know now
I'd have gone around Cape Horn.

The women have the hardest time
Who emigrate by land;
For when they cook out in the wind
They're sure to burn their hand.
Then they scold their husbands round,
Get mad and spill the tea, —
I'd have thanked my stars if they'd not come
      out
Upon this bleak prairie.

'Most every night we put out guards
To keep the Indians off.
When night comes round some heads will ache,
And some begin to cough.
To be deprived of help at night,
You know is mighty hard,
But every night there's some one sick,
To keep from standing guard.

Then they're always talking of what they've
      got,
And what they're going to do;
Some will say they're content,
For I've got as much as you.
Others will say, "I'll buy or sell,
I'm damned if I care which."
Others will say, "Boys, buy him out,
For he does n't own a stitch."

Old raw-hide shoes are hell on corns
While tramping through the sands,
And driving a jackass by the tail —
Damn the overland,
I would as leaf be on a raft at sea,
And there at once be lost.
John, let's leave the poor old mule,
We'll never get him across.

THE CAMP-FIRE HAS GONE OUT

Author unknown. First heard this sung in San Andreas Mountains. I think it was by 'Gene Rhodes.

Through progress of the railroads our occupation's
    gone;
So we will put ideas into words, our words into a
    song.
First comes the cowboy; he is pointed for the west;
Of all the pioneers I claim the cowboys are the best;
You will miss him on the round-up; it's gone, his
    merry shout, —
The cowboy has left the country and the camp-fire
    has gone out.

There is the freighters, our companions; you've
    got to leave this land;
Can't drag your loads for nothing through the
    gumbo and the sand.
The railroads are bound to beat you when you do
    your level best;
So give it up to the grangers and strike out for the
    west.

Bid them all adieu and give the merry shout, —
The cowboy has left the country and the camp-fire
    has gone out.

When I think of those good old days, my eyes with
    tears do fill;
When I think of the tin can by the fire and the coyote
    on the hill.
I'll tell you, boys, in those days old-timers stood a
    show, —
Our pockets full of money, not a sorrow did we
    know.
But things have changed now; we are poorly clothed
    and fed.
Our wagons are all broken and our ponies 'most all
    dead.
Soon we will leave this country; you'll hear the
    angels shout,
"Oh, here they come to Heaven, the camp-fire has
    gone out."

CHASE OF THE O L C STEER

*Sent me from Ogalala, Wyoming. Anonymous. Signed
Miss* ——

    Did you ever hear of the O L C Steer,
    With widely flaring horns?
    He smashes the trees as he splits the breeze,
    And the Cowboy's rope he scorns.

    That O L C's fame it soon became
    Of camp-fire yarns the pet;
    "I'll stake my rocks that I get that ox,"
    Quoth Ray, "Who'll take my bet?

"Why, of course my Gray Buck horse
Will run on him," he said.
"Show me his track. I'll bring him back,
I'll bet, alive or dead."

Up Johnny spoke: "No brags I make;
Straight goods I give you now:
I'll put my string on anything
From a coyote to a cow."

Then up spoke Bob: "With this here job
You bet I'm going to cope;
Just you watch me if you want to see
How Texas punchers rope."

These cowboys three for modesty
Have always been well known;
For don't you know, unless they blow,
Their horns they'd not be blown?

Meanwhile the steer, devoid of fear,
Was trailing o'er the Mesa.
He sniffed the air; what did he care?
He knew he was a racer.

With firm intent on business bent
Three youth rode up the trail.
The steer he saw and dropped his jaw,
And then he whisked his tail.

The other day I chanced that way:
That steer was grinning yet.
Six weeks have passed; not yet the last
Of why that steer they did n't get.

If they once begin, for hours they'll chin,
And tell, although they hit him
And ran all day, how he got away,
And why they did n't git 'im.

CHOPO

By N. Howard Thorp

Written in Devil's River, Texas, 1901, at Jeneaw, or Juno, Lake, when in camp with Frank Wilson. This little horse I got from Antelope George at Sierra Blanca, was branded O. I rode him from Sierra Blanca to Paris, Texas. This song was in my first publication, copyrighted in 1908.

Through rocky arroyos so dark and so deep;
Down the sides of the mountains so slippery and
      steep;
You've good judgment, sure-footed, wherever you
      go
You're a safety conveyance, my little Chopo.

Whether single or double, or in lead of a team,
Over highways or byways or crossing a stream,
You're always in fix and willing to go
Whenever you're called on, my Chico Chopo.

You're a good roping horse; you were never jerked
      down;
When tied to a steer, you will circle him around;
Let him once cross the string, and over he'll go.
You sabe the business, my cow horse Chopo.

One day on the Llano, a hail-storm began;
The herds were stampeded, the horses all ran;

The lightning it glittered, a cyclone did blow;
But you faced the sweet music, my little Chopo.

Chopo, my pony; Chopo, my pride;
Chopo, my amigo; Chopo I will ride
From Mexico's border 'cross Texas Llanos;
To the salt Pecos River I ride you, Chopo.

CHUCK-TIME ON THE ROUND-UP

By Austin Corcoran, Grand Junction, Colorado

*I first heard it sung at Monte Vista, Colorado, by Jack
Brenner.*

It was chuck-time on the round-up, and we heard
    "Old Doughy" shout —
"You had better come and get this or I'll throw the
    whole thing out."
So we headed for the wagon like wild stampeded herd,
Fearful every minute lest the cook might keep his
    word.

The way we gathered round that mess-box, scram-
    blin' for tools,
Showed the disregard for ethics that is taught in
    other schools;
But what we lacked in manners we made up in
    friendly strife,
To see who'd get through quickest with the stuff
    that prolongs life.

And "Old Doughy" stood and watched us with the
    pot-hook in his hands
That he used for liftin' covers from the pots and
    fryin'-pans;

And also used to carry out remarks he'd sometimes
    make
To any thoughtless rider who, in fear of bein' late,
Would ride too near the pot-rack and start a lot of
    dust
That would settle in his kitchen 'til "Cooke's"
    rage would bust.

For "Doughy" is particular — that is all there is to
    that;
But when it comes to sour-dough bread, we all
    take off our hat
To him, and swear that no matter where you'd
    a mind to look,
You'd never find man to equal "Old Doughy"
    with the hook.

And when it comes to feedin' men — that is, so
    they'll stay fed —
And spend their nights in slumber 'stead o' wres-
    tlin' with the bed,
Your city chef can learn a lot from our old round-up
    cook,
Who never learned a thing he knows from recipes
    or book,
But just practiced on us fellows 'til he learnt all
    there is to know
About this cookin' business and mixin' sour dough.

Oh! There's many ways of dinin', from what I've
    read and heard,
From meals that's served in courses to a "bottle
    and a bird";

But when it comes to eatin' stuff that tasted good
　　all the way,
I would n't quit a mess-box for a Broadway café.

For when he slides the hooks along the pot-rack,
　　piles on wood,
And while the fire is burnin' down starts mixin'
　　somethin' good,
An' you just keep a-lookin' 'til your eyes begin to
　　ache,
And wonder what new kind of dish "Old Doughy"
　　's goin' to make.
He puts in raisins, sugar, currants, and a lot of other
　　stuff,
'Til all at once you realize you're goin' to have
　　"plum duff."

Now I reckon in the cities they'd spell that word in
　　French,
'Til you would n't know just what they meant —
　　a latigo or cinch —
And you'd be none the wiser when they set it by
　　your plate,
Nor, after it was eaten could you swear to what
　　you ate?

In fact you would n't know 'til mornin' that you
　　had really dined
And taken in a lot of stuff your in'ards couldn't grind.
But you get the first reminder along about "last
　　guard,"
When that "Frenchy" stuff starts quarrelin' down
　　in your "front yard,"

Somethin' like the cattle that start to "millin'" in
    the night,
And try to quit their bed-ground at some imaginary
    fright.

But unlike the friendly "Dogies," you can't sing
    this stuff to sleep,
For all the music that goes with it was furnished
    while you eat.
An' perhaps it's just as well, for you could n't sing
    a note
With all that sorrow in your pantry and that burnin'
    in your throat
That is caused by too much vintage of celebrated
    make,
Which early in the evenin' you thought so nice to take;
But later showed developments which led you to
    believe
That the stuff was manufactured from a kind of
    "loco weed";

Then you recall the bottles that were stored away
    so nice,
With some blankets wrapped around 'em in a bucket
    of cracked ice,
With their golden yellow labels like the "Dogies"
    from Old Mex,
And you know it 's somethin' extra by the figures on
    your checks.

But it differs from those "Dogies" that have crossed
    the Rio Grande,
For you cannot tell the value by the color or the brand.

So you have to take your chances on what
    "Frenchy" minds to serve,
And try to catch the bedpost as it comes around the
    curve;
Then commence an awful tussle when you try to
    ride the bunk,
While the "wireless" keeps you posted on the
    "doin' down in front."

For you keep a-hearin' rumors of an international
    riot,
Caused by the cost of higher livin' on this purely
    foreign diet,
'Til you are forced to take some issue in the trouble
    near at hand,
And try to organize your forces to make a final
    stand
Against this food combine that has got you in its grip,
'Til you think you're in the stateroom of an ocean-
    goin' ship.

That seems to take you further from the scenes you
    recognize,
And you get to wonderin' how it feels when a fellow
    really dies.
Still you keep on hearin' echoes of last night's food
    and song,
'Til you realize it's mornin' and the "Frenchy
    Revolution's" on.
Of course you may recover, and perhaps you're
    none the worse,
But for me there's no "swell" eatin' while
    "Frenchy" drives the hearse.

Oh! You who dine in cities, passing through plate-
    glass doors,
Winding in around swell tables set on polished
    marble floors,
Followin' a darky who will show you to your seat,
While one will take your hat and another brush
    your feet —
Dinin' with fair ladies while sweet music fills the
    room,
And you gladly tip the "leader" for the lady's
    favorite tune;

You who linger long and listen to the things you like
    to hear
In the swell cafés in cities that to you are always
    dear,
May think that I am partial to the "cowboy" and
    his "grub,"
But I've dined at all those cafés and was fed once
    at a club,
And I've come to this conclusion, and right here
    I want to say,
When you eat at "Café Doughy's" you feel all
    right next day,
For here is "Doughy's" record, and beat it if you
    can —
He's cooked for us for twenty years and never lost
    a man.

A COW-CAMP ON THE RANGE

Authorship credited to Tom Mew, Oklahoma. First heard it sung by Walker Hyde, Three Rivers, New Mexico.

Oh, the prairie dogs are barking,
And the birds are on the wing,
See the heel fly chase the heifers, boys! —
'T is a first-class sign of spring.
The elm wood is budding,
The earth is turning green;
See the pretty things of nature,
That make life a pleasant dream!

I'm just living through the winter
To enjoy the coming change,
For there is no place so homelike
As a cow-camp on the range.
The boss is smiling sum'tious,
Radiant as the setting sun;
But we know he ain't contented,
For he ain't a-cussin' none.

The cook is at the chuck-box
Whistling "Heifers in the Green,"
Making baking-powder biscuits, boys,
While the pot is biling beans.
The boys untie their bedding
And unroll it on the run,
For they are in a monstrous hurry,
For the supper's almost done.

"Chuck is ready — come en get it!"
Cried the cook's familiar voice

As he climbed the wagon wheel
To watch the cowboys all rejoice.
Then all thoughts were turned with reverence
To a plate of beef and beans,
As we grazed on beef and biscuits
Like yearlings on the range.

To the hot place with your city,
Where they herd like frightened rats
On a range so badly crowded
There ain't room to cuss a cat.
This life is not so sum'tious,
I'm not longing for a change,
But there is no place so homelike
As a cow-camp on the range.

THE COWBOY AT CHURCH

*Author unknown to me, but my hat off to him, whoever
he may be. Heard it recited by a young high-school girl
at Montrose, Colorado.*

Some time ago — two weeks or more
If I remember well —
I found myself in town, and thought
I'd knock around a spell;
When all at once I heard the bell —
I did n't know 't was Sunday,
For on the plains we scarcely know
A Sunday from a Monday —

A-calling all the people
From the highways and the hedges,
And all the reckless throng
That tread ruin's ragged edges,

To come and hear the pastor tell
Salvation's touching story,
And how the new road misses hell
And leads you straight to glory.

I started by the chapel door,
But something urged me in,
And told me not to spend God's day
In revelry and sin.
I don't go much on sentiment,
But tears came to my eyes.
It seemed just like my mother's voice
Was speaking from the skies.

I thought how often she had gone
With little Sis and me
To church when I was but a lad,
'Way back in Tennessee.
It never once occurred to me
About not being dressed
In Sunday rig; but carelessly
I went in with the rest.

You should have seen the smiles and shrugs
As I went walking in,
As though they thought my leggins
Worse than any kind of sin;
Although the honest parson,
In his vestry garb arrayed,
Was dressed the same as I was —
In the trappings of his trade.

The good man prayed for all the world
And all its motley crew,

For pagan, Hindoo, sinners, Turk,
And unbelieving Jews, —
Though the congregation doubtless thought
That the cowboy as a race
Were a kind of moral outlaw
With no good claim to grace.

Is it very strange that cowboys are
A rough and reckless crew,
When their garb forbids their doing right
As Christian people do?
That they frequent scenes of revelry
Where death is bought and sold,
Where at least they get a welcome,
Though it's prompted by their gold?

Stranger, did it ever strike you,
When the winter days are gone,
And the mortal grass is springing up
To meet the judgment sun,
And we 'tend mighty round-ups
Where, according to the Word,
The angel cowboy of the Lord
Will cut the human herd —

That a heap of stock, that's lowing now
Around the Master's pen
And feeding at his fodder stack,
Will have the brand picked then?
A brand that when the hair was long
Looked like the letter C,
Will prove to be the devil's
And the brand the letter D;

While many a long-horned puncher —
I mean just so to speak —
That has n't had the advantage
Of the range and gospel creek
Will get to crop the grasses
In the pasture of the Lord
If the letter C showed up
Beneath the devil's checker-board?

THE COWBOY AT WORK

Heard this song sung at a cow-camp in Rocky Arroyo,
Eddy County, New Mexico.

You may call the cowboy horned and think him
    hard to tame,
You may heap vile epithets upon his head;
But to know him is to like him, notwithstanding his
    hard name,
For he will divide with you his beef and bread.

If you see him on his pony as he scampers o'er the
    plain,
You would think him wild and woolly to be sure;
But his heart is warm and tender when he sees a
    friend in need,
Though his education is but to endure.

When the storm breaks in its fury and lightning's
    vivid flash
Makes you thank the Lord for shelter and for bed,
Then it is he mounts his pony and away you see him
    dash,
No protection but the hat upon his head.

Such is life upon a cow-ranch and the half was
    never told;
But you never find a kinder-hearted set
Than the cattleman at home, be he either young or
    old;
He's a "daisy from away back," don't forget.

When you fail to find a pony or a cow that's gone
    astray,
Be that cow or pony wild or be it tame,
The cowboy, like the drummer, — and the bed-
    bug, too, they say, —
Bring him to you, for he gets there just the same.

THE COWBOYS' CHRISTMAS BALL

By Larry Chittenden, of Texas

*I received this song from Miss Jessie Forbes, at Eddy,
New Mexico, 1898. I understand it was one of a collection
of Chittenden's entitled Ranch Verse.*

'Way out in Western Texas, where the Clear Fork's
    waters flow,
Where the cattle are a-browsin' and the Spanish
    ponies grow;
Where the Northers come a-whistlin' from beyond
    the Neutral Strip;
And the prairie dogs are sneezin', as though they
    had the grip;
Where the coyotes come a-howlin' round the
    ranches after dark,
And the mockin' birds are singin' to the lovely
    medder lark;

Where the 'possum and the badger and the rattle-
    snakes abound,
And the monstrous stars are winkin' o'er a wilder-
    ness profound;
Where lonesome, tawny prairies melt into airy
    streams,
While the Double Mountains slumber in heavenly
    kinds of dreams;
Where the antelope is grazin' and the lonely plovers
    call,
It was there I attended the Cowboys' Christmas
    Ball.

The town was Anson City, old Jones' county seat,
Where they raised Polled Angus cattle and waving
    whiskered wheat;
Where the air is soft and bammy and dry and full
    of health,
Where the prairies is explodin' with agricultural
    wealth;
Where they print the Texas Western, that Hall
    McCann supplies
With news and yarns and stories, of most amazin'
    size;
Where Frank Smith "pulls the badger" on knowin'
    tenderfeet,
And Democracy's triumphant and mighty hard to
    beat;
Where lives that good old hunter, John Milsap,
    from Lamar,
Who used to be the sheriff "back east in Paris,
    sah."

'T was there, I say, at Anson with the lovely Widder
   Wall,
That I went to that reception, the Cowboys' Christ-
   mas Ball.

The boys had left the ranches and come to town in
   piles;
The ladies, kinder scatterin', had gathered in for
   miles.
And yet the place was crowded, as I remember
   well,
'T was gave on this occasion at the Morning Star
   Hotel.
The music was a fiddle and a lively tambourine,
And viol came imported, by the stage from Abilene.
The room was togged out gorgeous — with mistle-
   toe and shawls,
And the candles flickered festious, around the airy
   walls.
The wimmen folks looked lovely — the boys looked
   kinder treed,
Till the leader commenced yellin', "Whoa, fellers,
   let's stampede,"
And the music started sighin' and a-wailin' through
   the hall
As a kind of introduction to the Cowboys' Christ-
   mas Ball.

The leader was a feller that came from Thompson's
   ranch,
They called him Windy Billy from Little Deadman's
   Branch.

His rig was kinder keerless, big spurs and high‹
    heeled boots;
He had the reputation that comes when fellers
    shoots.
His voice was like a bugle upon the mountain
    height;
His feet were animated and a mighty movin' sight,
When he commenced to holler, "Now, fellers
    stake your pen.
Lock horns ter all them heifers and rustle them like
    men;
Saloot yer lovely critters; now swing and let 'em go;
Climb the grapevine round 'em; now all hands do-
    ce-do.
You maverick, jine the round-up, jess skip the
    waterfall,"
Huh, hit was gettin' active, the Cowboys' Christ-
    mas Ball.

The boys was tol'able skittish, the ladies powerful
    neat;
That old brass viol's music just got there with both
    feet;
That wailin', frisky fiddle, I never shall forget;
And Windy kept a-singin' — I think I hear him
    yet —
"Oh, yes, chase yer squirrels an cut 'em to our side;
Spur Treadwell to the center, with Cross P Char-
    ley's bride;
Doc Hollis down the center, and twine the ladies'
    chain;
Van Andrews, pen the fillies in big T Diamond's
    train.

All pull your freight together, now swallow fork and
    change;
Big Boston, lead the trail herd through little Pitch-
    fork's range.
Purr round yer gentle pussies, now rope and bal-
    ance all."
Huh, hit were gettin' active — the Cowboys' Christ-
    mas Ball.

The dust riz fast and furious; we all jes' galloped
    round,
Till the scenery got so giddy that T Bar Dick was
    downed.
We buckled to our pardners and told 'em to hold
    on,
Then shook our hoofs like lightnin' until the early
    dawn.
Don't tell me 'bout cotillions, or germans — no,
    sir-ee!
That whirl at Anson City jes' takes the cake with
    me.
I'm sick of lazy shufflin's, of them I've had my
    fill;
Give me a frontier break-down backed up by Windy
    Bill.
McAllister ain't nowhere, when Windy leads the
    show;
I've seen 'em both in harness, and so I ought ter
    know.
Oh, Bill, I shan't forget yer, and I oftentimes
    recall
That lively gaited sworray — the Cowboys' Christ-
    mas Ball.

THE COWBOY'S DREAM

*Given me by Wait Roberts, Double Diamond Ranch,
White Mountains, 1898. Authorship ascribed to father
of Captain Roberts, of the Texas Rangers.*

Last night, as I lay on the prairie,
And looked at the stars in the sky,
I wondered if ever a cowboy
Would drift to that sweet by and by.

I hear there's to be a grand round-up
Where cowboys with others must stand,
To be cut out by the riders of judgment
Who are posted and know all the brands.

The trail to that great mystic region
Is narrow and dim, so they say;
While the one that leads down to perdition
Is posted and blazed all the way.

Whose fault is it, then, that so many
Go astray, on this wild range fail,
Who might have been rich and had plenty
Had they known of the dim, narrow trail?

I wonder if at the last day some cowboy
Unbranded and unclaimed should stand,
Would he be mavericked by those riders of judgment
Who are posted and know all the brands?

I wonder if ever a cowboy
Stood ready for that Judgment Day,
And could say to the Boss of the Riders,
"I'm ready, come, drive me away"?

For they, like the cows that are locoed,
Stampede at the sight of a hand,
Are dragged with a rope to the round-up,
Or get marked with some crooked man's brand.

And I'm scared that I'll be a stray yearling,
A maverick, unbranded on high,
And get cut in the bunch with the "rusties"
When the Boss of the Riders goes by.

For they tell of another big owner
Who's ne'er overstocked, so they say,
But who always makes room for the sinner
Who drifts from the straight, narrow way.

They say he will never forget you,
That he knows every action and look;
So for safety you'd better get branded,
Have your name in the great Tally Book.

My wish for all cowboys is this:
That we may meet at that grand final sale;
Be cut out by the riders of judgment
And shoved up the dim, narrow trail.

THE COWBOY'S LAMENT

Authorship credited to Troy Hale, Battle Creek, Nebraska. I first heard it sung in a bar-room at Wisner, Nebraska, about 1886.

As I walked out in the streets of Laredo,
As I walked out in Laredo one day,
I spied a poor cowboy wrapped up in white linen,
Wrapped up in white linen as cold as the clay.

"Oh, beat the drum slowly and play the fife lowly,
Play the Dead March as you bear me along;
Take me to the graveyard, and lay the sod over me,
For I'm a young cowboy, and I know I've done
    wrong.

"I see by your outfit that you are a cowboy," —
These words he did say as I boldly stepped by —
"Come, sit beside me and hear my sad story;
I was shot in the breast and I know I must die.

"Let sixteen gamblers come handle my coffin,
Let sixteen cowboys come sing me a song,
Take me to the graveyard and lay the sod over me,
For I'm a poor cowboy, and I know I've done wrong.

"My friends and relations they live in the Nation,
They know not where their boy has gone.
He first came to Texas and hired to a ranchman,
Oh, I'm a young cowboy, and I know I've done
    wrong.

"Go write a letter to my gray-haired mother,
And carry the same to my sister so dear;
But not a word shall you mention
When a crowd gathers round you my story to
    hear.

"There is another more dear than a sister,
She'll bitterly weep when she hears I am gone.
There is another who will win her affections,
For I'm a young cowboy, and they say I've done
    wrong.

"Go gather around you a crowd of young cowboys,
And tell them the story of this my sad fate;
Tell one and the other before they go further
To stop their wild roving before 't is too late.

"Oh, muffle your drums, then play your fifes mer-
rily;
Play the Dead March as you bear me along.
And fire your guns right over my coffin;
There goes an unfortunate boy to his home.

"It was once in the saddle I used to go dashing,
It was once in the saddle I used to be gay;
First to the dram-house, then to the card-house:
Got shot in the breast, I am dying to-day.

"Get six jolly cowboys to carry my coffin;
Get six pretty maidens to bear up my pall;
Put bunches of roses all over my coffin,
Put roses to deaden the clods as they fall.

"Then swing your rope slowly and rattle your spurs
lowly,
And give a wild whoop as you bear me along;
And in the grave throw me, and roll the sod over
me,
For I'm a young cowboy, and I know I've done
wrong.

"Go bring me a cup, a cup of cold water,
To cool my parched lips," the cowboy said;
Before I turned, the spirit had left him
And gone to its Giver — the cowboy was dead.

We beat the drum slowly and played the fife lowly,
And bitterly wept as we bore him along;
For we all loved our comrade, so brave, young, and
  handsome;
We all loved our comrade, although he'd done
  wrong.

THE COWBOY'S LIFE

*Heard this sung at a little round-up at Seven Lakes,
New Mexico, by a puncher named Spence.*

> The bawl of a steer
> To a cowboy's ear
> Is music of sweetest strain;
> And the yelping notes
> Of the gray coyotes
> To him are a glad refrain.
>
> And his jolly songs
> Speed him along
> As he thinks of the little gal
> With golden hair
> Who is waiting there
> At the bars of the home corral.
>
> For a kingly crown
> In the noisy town
> His saddle he would n't change;
> No life so free
> As the life we see
> 'Way out on the Yaso range.
>
> His eyes are bright
> And his heart as light

As the smoke of his cigarette;
There's never a care
For his soul to bear,
No trouble to make him fret.

The rapid beat
Of his bronco's feet,
On the sod as he speeds along,
Keeps living time
To the ringing rhyme
Of his rollicking cowboy's song.

Hike it, cowboys,
For the range away
On the back of a bronc of steel,
With a careless flirt
Of the raw-hide quirt
And the dig of a roweled heel.

The winds may blow
And the thunder growl
Or the breeze may safely moan;
A cowboy's life
Is a royal life,
His saddle his kingly throne.

Saddle up, boys,
For the work is play
When love's in the cowboy's eyes,
When his heart is light
As the clouds of white
That swim in the summer skies.

THE COWBOY'S MEDITATION

I regret that I do not know the author's name. Have tried to locate him, but so far have failed. Heard this sung in Bluff City, Utah, by an old puncher named Carter.

At midnight, when the cattle are sleeping,
On my saddle I pillow my head,
And up at the heavens lie peeping
From out of my cold grassy bed; —
Often and often I wondered,
At night when lying alone,
If every bright star up yonder
Is a big peopled world like our own.

Are they worlds with their ranges and ranches?
Do they ring with rough-rider refrains?
Do the cowboys scrap there with Comanches
And other Red Men of the plains?
Are the hills covered over with cattle
In those mystic worlds far, far away?
Do the ranch-houses ring with the prattle
Of sweet little children at play?

At night, in the bright stars up yonder,
Do the cowboys lie down to their rest?
Do they gaze at this old world and wonder
If rough riders dash over its breast?
Do they list to the wolves in the canyons?
Do they watch the night owl in its flight,
With their horses their only companions
While guarding the herd through the night?

Sometimes, when a bright star is twinkling
Like a diamond set in the sky,

I find myself lying and thinking,
It may be God's heaven is nigh.
I wonder if there I shall meet her,
My mother whom God took away;
If in the star-heavens I'll greet her
At the round-up that's on the Last Day.

In the east the great daylight is breaking,
And into my saddle I spring;
The cattle from sleep are awaking,
The heaven-thoughts from me take wing;
The eyes of my bronco are flashing,
Impatient he pulls at the reins,
And off round the herd I go dashing,
A reckless cowboy of the plains.

A COWBOY'S PRAYER

*Given me by Phil LeNoir, Secretary of the Las Vegas
Round-Up. Afterwards found it in Charles Badger
Clark, Jr.'s, book, "Sun and Saddle Leather."*

O Lord, I ain't never lived where churches grow.
I like creation better as it stood
That day You finished it so long ago
And looked upon Your work and called it good
I know that others find You in the light
That's sifted down through tinted window-panes,
And yet I seem to feel You near to-night
In this dim, quiet starlight on the plains.

I thank You, Lord, that I am placed so well,
That You have made my freedom so complete;
That I'm no slave of whistle, clock, or bell,
Nor weak-eyed prisoner of wall and street.

Just let me live my life as I've begun
And give me work that's open to the sky;
Make me a pardner of the wind and sun
And I won't ask a life that's soft or high.

Let me be easy on the man that's down;
Let me be square and generous with all.
I'm careless, sometimes, Lord, when I'm in town,
But never let 'em say I'm mean or small!
Make me as big and open as the plains,
As honest as the horse between my knees,
Clean as the wind that blows behind the rains,
Free as the hawk that circles down the breeze.

Forgive me, Lord, if sometimes I forget.
You know about the reasons that are hid.
You understand the things that gall and fret;
Why, You know me better than my mother did!
Just keep an eye on all that's done and said,
Just right me sometimes when I turn aside,
And lead me on that long dim trail ahead
That stretches upward toward the Great Divide.

A COWBOY'S PRIZE

Published in "Denver Post." I first heard it sung by Al Roberts in White Oaks, New Mexico.

Never was no gal like Mollie
In creation, I don't think!
Hotter'n a hot tamale;
Han'some ain't the word to fit 'er —
She's a beauty head to heel —
Lightnin'-built git-up-an'-gitter,
An' as true as polished steel.

Case o' love at first sight, reckon —
On my part, you understand —
An' I swore she'd soon be packin'
This same ol' cow-puncher's brand.
Went into the game an' won 'er,
From all rivals yanked the prize;
Cut 'er from the bunch an' run 'er
Off before their jealous eyes.

Now she's mine. There ain't a prouder
Rider on the ranges, see?
Mortal could n't yawp no louder
Crackin' up her worth than me.
From the crupper to the snaffle
She's a thorrerbred, that mare,
That I won at Johnson's raffle
At the T ranch on the Bear.

COWBOYS VICTIMIZED

By James Barton Adams

I first heard this song in El Paso, Texas, at a Stock Association meeting, sung between supper and breakfast by a man with a good voice, and long afterwards learned the author's name.

We had all made the guess by the cut of his dress
     an' the tenderfoot style that he slung,
An' the way that he spun toney language that run
     slick as grease from the p'int of his tongue,
That he was a red-hotter from over the water, a juke
     or a markis, or wuss,
Than that in his rank, an' we thought we could bank
     on havin' some fun with the cuss.

He talked with a drawl till his words seemed to fall
    reluctant outen his mouth,
An' the babyish stare in his eyes you would swear
    showed a brain that was stunted by drouth;
An' the boys o' the range all regarded the strange
    sort o' cuss that had come there to board
For his health as a snob an' we put up a job that'd
    lower the pride o' my lord.

He remarked that he could ride anything that wore
    hide; he had rid with the 'ounds, don't ye
    know;
An' we told him we thought we'd be able to trot out
    a hoss that wa'n't fashioned for show —
One o' kittenish views that'd serve to amuse of his
    highness if he was inclined
Fur to try it a whirl, an' he smiled like a girl, an'
    would ride it if we did n't mind.
An' he went farther with an offer to bet all the
    boodle that we could perduce,
That he'd ride anything we'd a notion to bring till
    he toned it down tame as a goose.
An' in manner quite rash our available cash was
    flashed fur to back up our views
That we'd find him a chunk of quick-action bronc
    that'd buck him plumb outen his shoes!

We'd a mare in the herd that was reckoned a bird,
    jest a bundle o' git-up-an'-git;
Half devil, half hoss, which the same is a cross
    that's productive o' meanness an' grit;
She had downed every rider that dared get astride
    her and crippled a dozen or so

Of the fellows who'd said that the hoss was n't
    bred that could give 'em the wust of a go;
So we saddled ol' Satan, the tenderfoot waitin'
    with a grin on his innercent face;
An' we got him astraddle an' sot in the saddle an'
    seed everything was in place,
An' we bid him good-bye with a wink o' the eye at
    each other an' anxiously stood
Holdin' onto the head o' the bronc till he said we
    might let 'er go if we would.

If the heavens had fell all around that corral an'
    drowned us in clouds from the skies
I kin tell you, by gad, that we would n't 'a' had any
    bigger a bunch o' surprise;
Fur he sot in his seat in the saddle as neat as if
    lollin' around in a chair,
An' that bronco a-thumpin' the earth an' a-jumpin'
    in spasms right up in the air;
Lit a cigarette right in the heat o' the fight an'
    grinned at the animal's jumps,
Us guys standin' there with a paralyzed stare like
    a bunch o' half-idiot chumps;
An' I'm tellin' you, boss, that he stayed with that
    hoss until he got it as meek as a calf,
An' rid it around on the hoof-battered ground an'
    givin' us fellers the laugh!

Every devilish bloke in the gang had gone broke
    a-backin' his honest belief
That the bronco we'd picked that had never been
    licked 'd sure bring the stranger to grief;
An' we bellered an' swore till our lungs was plum

sore when we learned that the schemin'
young hound
Was Bronco Bill Snyder, the champion rider,
a-huntin' a snap — which he found.

THE COWMAN'S PRAYER

*Don't know the author's name. Heard it sung in a cow-
camp near Fort Sumner, on the Pecos River, New
Mexico.*

Now, O Lord, please lend me thine ear,
The prayer of a cattleman to hear;
No doubt the prayers may seem strange,
But I want you to bless our cattle range.

Bless the round-ups year by year,
And don't forget the growing steer;
Water the lands with brooks and rills
For my cattle that roam on a thousand hills.

Prairie fires, won't you please stop?
Let thunder roll, water drop.
It frightens me to see the smoke;
Unless it's stopped, I'll go dead broke.

As you, O Lord, my herd behold,
It represents a sack of gold;
I think at least five cents a pound
Will be the price of beef the year round.

One thing more and then I'm through, —
Instead of one calf, give my cows two.
I may pray different from other men,
But I've had my say, and now, Amen.

THE CROOKED TRAIL TO HOLBROOK

*Mailed me from Douglas, Arizona, by an old friend
named Cotton.*

Come, all you jolly cowboys that follow the bronco
     steer,
I'll sing to you a verse or two your spirits for to
     cheer;
It's all about a trip that I did undergo
On that crooked trail to Holbrook, in Arizona, oh.

It was on the seventeenth of February our herd
     it started out,
It would have made your hearts jump to hear them
     bawl and shout,
As wild as any buffalo that ever swam the Platte,
Those cattle we were driving and every one was
     fat.

We crossed the Mescal Mountains on the way to
     Hidalgo,
And when we got to Gilson Flats, Lord, how the
     wind did blow!
But our spirits never failed us as onward we did go, —
On that crooked trail to Holbrook, in Arizona, oh.

That night we had a stampede; Lord, how the cattle
     run!
We made it to our horses; I tell you, we had fun;
Over the prickly pear and catclaw brush we quickly
     made our way;
We thought of our long journey and the girls we'd
     left one day.

It's long by Sombserva we slowly punched along,
While each and every puncher would sing a hearty
    song
To cheer up his comrade as onward we did go, —
On that crooked trail to Holbrook, in Arizona, oh.

We crossed the Mogollon Mountains where the tall
    pines grow,
Grass in abundance and rippling streams do flow;
Our packs were always turning, of course our gait
    was slow, —
On that crooked trail of Holbrook, in Arizona, oh.

At last we got to Holbrook — a little gale did blow;
It blew up sand and pebble stones, and it did n't
    blow them slow.
We had to drink the water from that muddy little
    stream,
And swallowed a peck of dirt when we tried to eat
    a bean.

But the cattle now are shipped and homeward we
    are bound
With a lot of as tired horses as ever could be
    found,
Across the reservation no danger did we fear,
But thought of wives and sweethearts and the ones
    we love so dear.

CROSSING THE DIVIDE

By J. W. Foley

One of the best of the lot. Heard this at a round-up in the Mogollon Mountains, sung by a puncher named Freckles.

Parson, I'm a maverick, just runnin' loose an'
    grazin',
Eatin' where's th' greenest grass an' drinkin' where
    I choose;
Had to rustle in my youth an' never had no raisin';
Was n't never halter broke an' I ain't much to lose;
Used to sleepin' in a bag an' livin' in a slicker;
Church folks never branded me — I don't know as
    they tried;
Wish you'd say a prayer for me an' try to make a
    dicker
For the best they'll give me when I cross the Big
    Divide.

Tell 'em I ain't corralled a night in more 'n twenty;
Tell 'em I'm rawboned an' rough an' ain't much for
    looks;
Tell 'em I don't need much grief because I've had
    a-plenty;
I don't know how bad I am 'cause I ain't kept no
    books.
Tell 'em I'm a maverick a-runnin' loose unbranded;
Tell 'em I shoot straight an' quick an' ain't got much
    to hide;
Have 'em come an' size me up as soon as I get
    landed,
For the best they'll give me when I cross the Great
    Divide.

Tell 'em I rode straight an' square an' never grabbed
    for leather;
Never roped a crippled steer or rode a sore-backed
    horse;
Tell 'em I've bucked wind an' rain an' every sort
    of weather,
Had my tilts with A. K. Hall an' Captain R. E.
    Morse.
Don't hide nothin' from 'em, whether it be sweet
    or bitter,
Tell 'em I'll stay on th' range, but if I'm shut
    outside
I'll abide it like a man because I ain't no
    quitter;
I ain't going to change just when I cross th' Big
    Divide.

Tell 'em, when th' Roundup comes for all us human
    critters,
Just corral me with my kind an' run a brand on
    me;
I don't want to be corralled with hypocrites an'
    quitters;
Brand me just for what I am — an' I'm just what
    you see.
I don't want no steam-het stall or bran-mash for
    my ration;
I just want to meet th' boss an' face him honest-
    eyed,
Show him just what chips I got an' shove 'em in for
    cashin';
That's what you can tell 'em when I cross the Big
    Divide.

DAN TAYLOR

Authorship credited to Len Doran, Mineral Wells,
Texas. I first heard it sung by Tom Williamson, while
carrying a bunch of horses from Monument Springs over
to Midland, Texas.

Dan Taylor is a rollicking cuss,
A frisky son of a gun;
He loves to court the maidens,
And he savvies how it's done.

He used to be a cowboy,
And they say he wasn't slow;
He could ride the bucking bronco
And swing the long lasso.

He could catch a maverick by the head
Or heel him on the fly;
He could pick up his front ones
Whenever he chose to try.

He used to ride 'most anything;
Now he seldom will.
He says they cut some caper in the air
Of which he's got his fill.

He is done and quit the business,
Settled down to quiet life,
And he's hunting for some maiden
Who will be his wife, —

One who will wash and patch his britches
And feed the setting hen,
Milk old Blue and Brindy,
And tend to baby Ben.

Then he'll build a cozy cottage
And furnish it complete,
He'll decorate the walls inside
With pictures new and sweet.

He will leave off riding broncos
And be a different man;
He will do his best to please his wife
In every way he can.

Then together in double harness
They will trot along down the line,
Until death shall call them over
To a bright and sunny clime.

May your joys be then completed
And your sorrows have an end,
Is the fondest wish of the writer, —
Your true and faithful friend.

A DEER HUNT

*There are several versions of this song. Everybody adds
a new verse. The author of this no one knows, as the
original song has been so changed by additions of verses
that there is little of it left.*

One pleasant summer day it came a storm of snow;
I picked my old gun and a-hunting I did go.

I came across a herd of deer and I trailed them
    through the snow;
I trailed them to the mountains where straight up
    they did go.

I trailed them o'er the mountains, I trailed them to
    the brim,
And trailed them to the waters where they jumped
    in to swim.

I cocked both my pistols and under water went, —
To kill the fattest of them deer, that was my whole
    intent.

While I was under water five hundred feet or more,
I fired both my pistols — like cannons did they roar.

I picked up my venison and out of water came, —
To kill the balance of them deer I thought it was my
    aim.

So I bent my gun in circles and fired round a hill,
And out of three or four deer ten thousand I did kill.

Then I picked up my venison and on my back I tied,
And as the sun came passing by I hopped up there
    to ride.

The sun she carried me o'er the globe; so merrily
    I did roam
That in four and twenty hours I landed safe at
    home.

And the money I received for my venison and skin,
I taken it all to the barn door and it would not all go in.

And if you doubt the truth of this I tell you how to
    know:
Just take my trail and go my rounds as I did long
    ago.

And if you get there before I do, and in case you do
    not find me,
I'll just back trail for a year or two, for the gal I left
    behind me.

DOWN ON THE OL' BAR-G

By Phil LeNoir

The boss he took a trip to France,
    Down on the ol' Bar-G.
He left his gal to run the ranch,
    Down on the ol' Bar-G.
She would n't let us chew nor cuss,
Had to keep slicked up like a city bus,
So round-up time was u-nan-i-mous,
    Down on the ol' Bar-G.

Our round-up cook he soon got th'u,
    Down on the ol' Bar-G.
Found his clay pipe right in the stew,
    Down on the ol' Bar-G.
But when we let that feller go
We married grief an' we married woe,
For the gal opined *she*'d bake the dough,
    Down on the ol' Bar-G.

Wisht you'd seen her openin' meal
    Down on the ol' Bar-G.
We all blinked twict — seemed plumb unreal,
    Down on the ol' Bar-G.
We had figs an' fudge an' whipped-up pru-in
An' angel-cake all dipped in goo-in,
"My Gawd," said Tex, "my stomick's ruin'"
    Down on the ol' Bar-G.

We quit that job an' cook-la-dee,
  Down on the ol' Bar-G.
An' pulled our freight for the lone prair-ee,
  Down on the ol' Bar-G.
For out on the range we could chew an' cuss
An' git real mean an' bois-ter-uss,
Whar apron-strings they could n't rope us,
  Down on the ol' Bar-G.

THE DREARY, DREARY LIFE

*An old song, a jumble of several. Authorship unknown.
I first heard it at Kingston, New Mexico, sung by a man
named Sam Jackson.*

A cowboy's life is a dreary, dreary life,
Some say it's free from care;
Rounding up the cattle from morning till night
On the bald prairie so bare.

Just about four o'clock old cook will holler out,
"Roll out, boys, it's almost day."
Through his broken slumbers the puncher he will ask,
Has the short summer night passed away?

The cowboy's life is a dreary, dreary life,
He's driven through the heat and cold;
While the rich man's a-sleeping on his velvet couch,
Dreaming of his silver and gold.

When the spring work sets in, then our troubles
      will begin,
The weather being fierce and cold;
We're almost froze, with the water on our clothes,
And the cattle we can scarcely hold.

The cowboy's life is a dreary, weary one,
He works all day to the setting of the sun;
And then his day's work is not done,
For there's his night guard to go on.

"Saddle up! Saddle up!" the boss will holler out,
When camped down by the Pecos Stream,
Where the wolves and owls with their terrifying howls
Will disturb us in our midnight dream.

You are speaking of your farms, you are speaking of
        your charms,
You are speaking of your silver and gold;
But a cowboy's life is a dreary, dreary life,
He's driven through the heat and cold.

Once I loved to roam, but now I stay at home:
All you punchers take my advice;
Sell your bridle and your saddle, quit your roaming
        and your travels,
And tie on to a cross-eyed wife.

THE DYING COWBOY

*Authorship credited to H. Clemons, Deadwood, Dakota,
1872. I first heard it from Kearn Carico, at Norfolk,
Nebraska, in 1886.*

"Oh, bury me not on the lone prairie";
Those words came slow and mournfully
From the pallid lips of a youth that lay
On his dying couch at the close of day.

He had wasted and pined till o'er his brow
Death's shadows fast were drawing now;
He had thought of home and the loved ones nigh,
As the cowboys gathered to see him die.

How oft have I listened to those well-known words,
The wild wind and the sound of birds;
He had thought of home and the cottonwood boughs,
Of the scenes that he loved in his childhood hours.

"I have always wished to be laid, when I died,
In the old churchyard on the green hillside,
By the grave of my father, oh, let my grave be;
Oh, bury me not on the lone prairie.

"I wish to be laid where a mother's care
And a sister's tear can mingle there;
Where friends can come and weep o'er me;
Oh, bury me not on the lone prairie.

"Oh, bury me not —" and his voice failed there;
They paid no heed to his dying prayer;
In a narrow grave just six by three,
They laid him there on the lone prairie.

Where the dewdrops fall and the butterfly rests,
The wild rose blooms on the prairie's crest,
Where the coyotes howl and the wind sports free,
They laid him there on the lone prairie.

THE END OF THE YAQUI TRAIL

By N. Howard Thorp

*Written while near Altar, in State of Sonora, old Mexico,
south of El Sarsabi, receiving a herd of steers for Allen
& Robinson, of the Lamy Grant, near Santa Fé, 1914.*

Living long lives in Sonora, nested 'mongst moun-
    tains high,
In close commune with the eagles that soar the
    Southern sky;

Living by hunting and fishing, raising their Indian
    corn,
High in the Sierra Madres, 't was there the Yaquis
    were born.

Loud in their childish prattle, playing with sticks
    and stones;
Each one a future warrior born to defend their
    homes;
Sons of Spartan mothers, reared in those mountains
    high,
Satisfied with a peaceful life just as you or I.

Crooning to their papooses just like your mam-
    mie or mine,
Squaws of a hardy nation, stoics and last of their
    line;
With every man's hand against them, driven from
    crag to fen,
God in His mercy defend them, for still they are
    mothers of men.

From the days of Don Velasquez, Alvarado, and
    Hernan Cortez,
Victoria Pednaza, Santana, and Porfirio Diaz,
They've driven them into slavery through Jalisco
    to Michoacan,
Through Guerrero Oaxaca Campeche to the jute-
    fields of Yucatan.

Save them till Montezuma, God of the Indian race,
Who, according to ancient tradition, shall some
    day come out of the East,

And call all the braves and warriors above and be-
    neath the sod
To rally around his standard and pay homage to
    their God.

THE FATE OF THE BEEF STEER
By J. W. Foley

*Heard this sung at a cow-camp at Solidad Ranch, New
Mexico.*

Hush-a-by, Long Horn, your pards are all sleepin';
Stop your durn millin' an' tossin' your head,
Wavin' your horns so unrestful, an' sweepin'
All of the beef herd with eyes big an' red.
Mebbe you know when you're pawin' the dust up,
Bellerin' ugly an' switchin' your tail;
Mebbe you know when you are nearin' the bust-up,
Nearin' the quittin' place — end of the trail.

Say, it's a queer trail that you've got to foller,
Scattered all over the face of the land,
All of you made into goods but the holler,
Part of you bottled an' part of you canned.
Wait till they're through with you till you knock
    under;
You've got so ticklish a journey to go.
All of the round-ups between here an' thunder
Could n't locate you, they'll scatter you so.

You think we crowd you — you'll have to go faster;
You ain't all steak — you'll discover that, too;
Wait till they put your red hair into plaster,
Boil down your hoofs into Stickum's Best Glue;

All of the grief in this world ain't bad weather;
Better lie down there an' take a short snooze.
Wait till they tan your tough hide into leather;
Wait till some feller is wearin' your shoes.

You don't know where you will have to go roamin',
What will be eatin' an' what will be worn;
Mebbe some woman in New York will be combin'
Out her back hair with a piece of your horn;
Mebbe the same time your tail will be travelin',
Cooked into soup for some tenderfoot's feed;
Some of your hide in a rope they'll be ravelin',
All of your innards gone on a stampede.

Better lie down there an' rest up, Ol' Ranger;
You ain't nigh come to the end of your trail;
Mebbe some woman, to you perfect stranger,
Will brush up crumbs with the end of your tail.
Don't pay to be too durn proud of your beller;
You ain't the only bad steer up north;
Wise to remember that no livin' feller
Ever can tell what a day will bring forth.

FIGHTIN' MAD

*Received from Miss Jean Beaumondy, Colorado Springs
Round-up, 1911. Jean was then the champion girl trick
roper of the world.*

I've swum the Colorado where she runs down close
        to hell;
I've braced the faro layouts at Cheyenne;
I've fought at muddy waters with a howling bunch
        of Sioux,
And I've eaten hot tamales in Cayenne.

I've rid a pitchin' bronco till the sky was under-
neath;
I've tackled every desert in the land;
I've sampled four X whiskey till I could n't hardly
see,
And I've dallied with the quicksands of the Grand.

I've argued with the marshals of a half-dozen burgs;
I've been drug free and fancy by a cow;
I've had three years' campaignin' with the fight-
in', bitin' Ninth;
But I never lost my temper till right now.

I've had the yellow fever, I've been plugged full of
holes,
I've grabbed an army mule plumb by its tail.
But I never was fightin', really downright fightin'
mad,
Till you ups and hands me that damn ginger ale.

FORGET THE EAST
By N. Howard Thorp

Oh, come en ride the Western range along with
Blue en me;
Forget your cares and worries — jest play you're
young en free.
You'll see the high Cliff Dwellings, built by a race
of old;
You'll see the Spanish diggin's, where the Padres
got their gold;
You'll see the Penitentes in their quaint religious
play,
Their crosses en Morada, in which they go to pray.

You'll see the Matachines in a dance that's all their
own;
The wild Comanches on horseback as they storm
a native home.
You'll find there's no restrictions on what you have
to do,
En scenes change like the seasons, each day brings
something new.
Wear old clothes, hunt, fish, en idle; do exactly as
you please,
Forget set rules en schedules — with a good horse
between your knees.

FRIJOLE BEANSES

By N. Howard Thorp

1919

I've cooked you in the strongest gypsum water;
I've boiled you up in water made of snow;
I've eaten you above the Arctic Circle,
I've chewed on you in southern Mexico.
In the camp-fire, on the stove, or in the oven,
Or buried in the ashes overnight,
You've saved my life on more than one occasion —
Oh, frijole bean, you're simply out of sight.

Of course you know, as far as one's digestion
Is concerned, you'd ever break it plumb in two
Without a single moment's hesitation —
Least that's the reputation given you.
Well here's to your health, you little brown frijole,
Your health I'll pledge and by you always stand;
You're eaten by the rich and by the lowly,
You're an outlawed product of our Western land.

Oh, little bean about you's such a savor,
Such a muchness, such a taste that you have got;
A particularly satisfying flavor
When we've added sow and chile to the pot.
Then good-bye, my little pard, I hate to leave you,
You've been with me on many a long hike;
So I'll eat the last of you that is in the skillet,
Then saddle up old buck and hit the pike.

THE GAL I LEFT BEHIND ME

*This song is so old that all the descendants of the author,
"I understand," have died of old age. I believe it was the
first cow song I ever heard.*

> I struck the trail in seventy-nine,
> The herd strung out behind me;
> As I jogged along my mind ran back
> For the gal I left behind me.
> That sweet little gal, that true little gal,
> The gal I left behind me!
>
> If ever I get off the trail
> And the Indians they don't find me,
> I'll make my way straight back again
> To the gal I left behind me.
> That sweet little gal, that true little gal,
> The gal I left behind me!
>
> The wind did blow, the rain did flow,
> The hail did fall and blind me;
> I thought of that gal, that sweet little gal,
> That gal I'd left behind me!
> That sweet little gal, that true little gal,
> The gal I left behind me!

She wrote ahead to the place I said,
I was always glad to find it;
She says, "I am true; when you get through,
Ride back and you will find me."
That sweet little gal, that true little gal,
The gal I left behind me!

When we sold out, I took the train,
I knew where I would find her;
When I got back we had a smack,
And that was no gol-darned liar.
That sweet little gal, that true little gal,
The gal I left behind me!

GET ALONG, LITTLE DOGIES

*Heard this song sung in Tombstone, Arizona, by Jim
Falls.*

As I walked out one morning for pleasure,
I spied a cow-puncher all riding alone;
His hat throwed back and his spurs was a-jinglin'
As he approached me a-singin' this song:

Whoopee ti yi yo, git along, little dogies,
It's your misfortune, and none of my own.
Whoopee ti yi yo, git along, little dogies,
For you know Wyoming will be your new home.

Early in the spring we round up the dogies,
Mark and brand and bob off their tails;
Round up our horses, load up the chuck-wagon,
Then throw the dogies upon the North trail.

It's whoopin' and yellin' and drivin' the dogies;
Oh, how I wish you would go on;
It's whoopin' and punchin', go on, little dogies,
For you know Wyoming will be your new home.

Some boys go up the trail for pleasure,
But that's where you get it most awfully wrong;
For you have n't an idea the trouble they give us
While we go drivin' them all along.

Your mother she was raised 'way down in Texas,
Where the jimson weed and sand-burrs grow;
Now we'll fill you up on prickly pear and cholla,
Till you are ready for the trail to Idaho.

Oh, you'll be soup for Uncle Sam's Injuns;
"It's beef, heap beef," I hear them cry.
Git along, git along, little dogies,
You're goin' to be beef steers by and by.

THE GOL-DARNED WHEEL

*Mailed me by a friend from Marfa, Texas, who heard it
sung by a cow-puncher named Hudspeth.*

I can take the wildest bronco in the tough old woolly
    West;
I can ride him, I can break him, let him do his level
    best;
I can handle any cattle who ever wore a coat of hair,
And I've had a lively russle with a tarnal grizzly
    bear;
I can rope and throw the longhorn of the wildest
    Texas brand,
And in Indian disagreements I can play a leading
    hand;

But at last I got my master, and he surely made me
    squeal,
When the boys got me a-straddle of that gol-darned
    wheel.

It was at the Eagle Ranch on the Brazos,
When I first found that darned contrivance that
    upset me in the dust.
A tenderfoot had brought it; he was wheeling all
    the way
From the sunrise end of freedom out to San Fran-
    cisco Bay.
He tied up at the ranch for to get outside a meal,
Never thinkin' we would monkey with his gol-
    darned wheel.

Arizona Jim begun it when he said to Jack McGill,
There was fellows forced to limit braggin' on their
    ridin' skill;
And he'd venture the admission the same fellow
    that he meant
Was a very handy critter far as ridin' broncos went;
But he would find that he was buckin' 'gainst a dif-
    ferent kind of deal
If he threw his leather leggins 'gainst a gol-darned
    wheel.

Such a slam against my talent made me hotter than
    a mink,
And I swore that I would ride him for amusement or
    for chink.
And it was nothin' but a plaything for the kids and
    such about,

And they'd have their ideas shattered if they'd lead
    the critter out.
They held it while I mounted and gave the word
    to go;
The shove they gave to start me warn't unreason-
    ably slow.
But I never spilled a cuss-word and I never spilled
    a squeal —
I was buildin' reputation on that gol-darned wheel.

Holy Moses and the Prophets how we split the
    Texas air,
And the wind it made whip-crackers of my same old
    canthy hair,
And sorta comprehended as down the hill we went
There was bound to be a smash-up that I could n't
    well prevent.
Oh, how them punchers bawled, "Stay with her,
    Uncle Bill!
Stick your spurs in her, you sucker, turn her muzzle
    up the hill!"
But I never made an answer; I just let the cusses
    squeal,
I was buildin' reputation on that gol-darned wheel.

The grade was mighty slopin' from the ranch down
    to the creek,
And I went a-galliflutin' like a crazy lightnin'
    streak —
Went whizzin' and a-dartin' first this way and then
    that,
The darned contrivance sort o' wobbling like the
    flyin' of a bat.

I pulled upon the handles, but I could n't check it up,
And I yanked and sawed and hollowed, but the
    darned thing would n't stop.
Then a sort of a thinker in my brain began to steal,
That the devil held a mortgage on that gol-darned
    wheel.

I've sort o' dim and hazy remembrance of the stop,
With the world a-goin' round and the stars all
    tangled up;
Then there came an intermission that lasted till I
    found
I was lyin' at the ranch with the boys all gathered
    round,
And a doctor was sewin' on the skin where it was
    ripped,
And old Arizona whispered, " Well, old boy, I guess
    you 're whipped."
And I told him I was busted from sombrero down
    to heel,
And he grinned and said, " You ought to see that
    gol-darned wheel."

GREASER JOE'S PLACE

From the " Denver Republican."

You kin brag of city caffeys and their trout from
    streams and lakes.
Of their meals served a la carty and their mush-
    rooms and their steaks;
But the grub at Greaser Joe's is the finest ever dealt:
Come, hombrey, and jest tuck a bowl of chile
    'neath your belt!

The music's kind o' skimpin' and it don't go very far;
It's dealt out by a half-breed and a mighty bad
    guitar;
But old Joe is a winner when it comes to mixin' dope,
And the first smell of his chile 'd give a dyin' hoss-
    thief hope.

There is sometimes rough stunts doin' and p'r'aps
    some powder burnt,
For the men who eat at Joe's all the p'litest ways
    ain't learnt;
But good food is like to most things that are scarce
    and hard to get —
It's worth some risk in trallin' and a-makin' yours,
    you bet!

So jest come with me to Joe's where there ain't no
    menu stunt,
Where the tablecloths is minus and a napkin's
    an affront,
And you'll get a bowl of chile that'll warm you
    through and through,
So come with me to Jose's, you tenderfoot — yes,
    you!

THE GREAT ROUND-UP

*I first heard this song sung by Sally White, at Toya,
Texas, in 1909, although a slightly different version was
published in my first edition of "Songs of the Cowboys."*

When I think of the last great round-up,
On the eve of eternity's dawn,
I think of the past of the cowboys
Who have been with us here and are gone.

And I wonder if any will greet me
On the sands of the evergreen shore
With a hearty, " God bless you, old fellow,"
That I've met with so often before.

I think of the big-hearted fellows
Who will divide with you, blanket and bread,
With a piece of stray beef well roasted,
And charge for it never a red.
I often look upward and wonder
If the green fields will seem half so fair,
If any the wrong trail have taken
And fail to " be in" over there.

For the trail that leads down to perdition
Is paved all the way with good deeds,
But in the great round-up of ages,
Dear boys, this won't answer your needs.
But the way to the green pastures, though narrow,
Leads straight to the home in the sky,
And Jesus will give you the passports
To the land of the sweet by and by.

For the Saviour has taken the contract
To deliver all those who believe,
At the headquarters ranch of His Father,
In the great range where none can deceive.
The Inspector will stand at the gateway
And the herd, one by one, will go by, —
The round-up by the angels in judgment
Must pass 'neath His all-seeing eye.

No maverick or slick will be tallied
In the great book of life in his home,
For he knows all the brands and the earmarks
That down through the ages have come.

But along with the tailings and sleepers
The strays must turn from the gate;
No road brand to gain them admission,
But the awful sad cry of "too late."

Yet I trust, in the last great round-up,
When the rider shall cut the big herd,
That the cowboys shall be represented
In the earmark and brand of the Lord;
To be shipped to the bright mystic regions
Over there in green pastures to lie,
And led by the crystal still waters,
In that home of the sweet by and by.

HELL IN TEXAS

This song was originally entitled " The Birth of New Mexico." I have five different versions of it. As each version is supposed to be by a different author, and I can only procure the names of three of them, I shall brand it as a "maverick" and let it go at that.

The Devil we're told in hell was chained,
And a thousand years he there remained;
He never complained nor did he groan,
But determined to start a hell of his own,
Where he could torment the souls of men
Without being chained in a prison pen.
So he asked the Lord if he had on hand.
Anything left when he made the land.

The Lord said, "Yes, I had plenty on hand
But I left it down on the Rio Grande;
The fact is, old boy, the stuff is so poor
I don't think you could use it in hell any more."

But the Devil went down to look at the truck,
And said if it came as a gift he was stuck;
For after examining it carefully and well,
He concluded the place was too dry for hell.

So in order to get it off his hands,
The Lord promised the Devil to water the lands;
For he had some water, or rather some dregs,
A regular cathartic that smelled like bad eggs.
Hence the deal was closed and the deed was given,
And the Lord went back to his home in heaven.
And the Devil then said, " I have all that is needed
To make a good hell," and hence he succeeded.

He began to put thorns in all of the trees,
And mixed up the sand with millions of fleas;
And scattered tarantulas along all the roads;
Put thorns on the cactus and horns on the toads.
He lengthened the horns of the Texas steers,
And put an addition on the rabbit's ears;
He put a little devil in the bronco steed,
And poisoned the feet of the centipede.

The rattlesnake bites you, the scorpion stings,
The mosquito delights you with buzzing wings;
The sand-burrs prevail, and so do the ants,
And those who sit down need half-soles on their
        pants.
The Devil then said that throughout the land
He'd managed to keep up the Devil's own brand,
And all would be mavericks unless they bore
The marks of scratches and bites and thorns by the
        score.

The heat in the summer is a hundred and ten,
Too hot for the Devil and too hot for men;
The wild boar roams through the black chaparral, —
It's a hell of a place he has for a hell!
The red pepper grows on the banks of the brooks;
The Mexicans use it in all that they cook.
Just dine with a Greaser, and then you will shout,
"I've hell on the inside as well as the out."

THE HELL-BOUND TRAIN

*Heard this sung at a cow-camp near Pontoon Crossing,
on the Pecos River, by a puncher named Jack Moore.*

A Texas cowboy lay down on a barroom floor,
Having drunk so much he could drink no more;
So he fell asleep with a troubled brain
To dream that he rode on a hell-bound train.

The engine with murderous blood was damp,
And was brilliantly lit with a brimstone lamp;
An imp for fuel was shoveling bones,
While the furnace rang with a thousand groans.

The boiler was filled with lager beer,
And the Devil himself was the engineer;
The passengers were a most motley crew, —
Church member, atheist, Gentile, and Jew;

Rich men in broadcloth, beggars in rags;
Handsome young ladies, withered old hags;
Yellow and black men, red, brown, and white,
All chained together, — O God, what a sight!

While the train rushed on at an awful pace,
The sulphurous fumes scorched their hands and
        face;
Wider and wider the country grew,
As faster and faster the engine flew.

Louder and louder the thunder crashed,
And brighter and brighter the lightning flashed;
Hotter and hotter the air became,
Till the clothes were burnt from each quivering
        frame.

And out of the distance there arose a yell,
"Ha, ha," said the Devil, "we're nearing hell!"
Then, oh, how the passengers shrieked with
        pain,
And begged the Devil to stop the train.

But he capered about and danced with glee,
And laughed and joked at their misery.
"My faithful friends, you have done the work,
And the Devil never can a payday shirk.

"You've bullied the weak, you've robbed the poor;
The starving brother you've turned from the door;
You've laid up gold where the canker rust,
And have given free vent to your beastly lust.

"You've justice scorned and corruption sown,
And trampled the laws of nature down;
You have drunk, rioted, cheated, plundered, and
        lied,
And mocked at God in your hell-born pride.

" You have paid full fare, so I'll carry you through;
For it's only right you should have your due.
Why, the laborer always expects his hire,
So I'll land you safe in the lake of fire —

" Where your flesh will waste in the flames that roar,
And my imps torment you forever more."
Then the cowboy awoke with an anguished cry,
His clothes wet with sweat and his hair standing high.

Then he prayed as he never had prayed till that
　　hour
To be saved from his sin and the demon's power.
And his prayers and his vows were not in vain;
For he never rode the hell-bound train.

HIGH-CHIN BOB

By Charles Badger Clark, Jr.

*This song was brought to Santa Fe by Henry Herbert
Knibbs, who got it from southern Arizona, where it was
sung by the cowboys. The song was written by Charles
Badger Clark, Jr., and the original version is in his " Sun
and Saddle Leather" under the title of " The Glory
Trail."*

'Way high up in the Mokiones, among the moun-
　　tain-tops,
A lion cleaned a yearlin's bones and licked his
　　thankful chops;
When who upon the scene should ride, a-trippin'
　　down the slope,
But High-Chin Bob of sinful pride and maverick-
　　hungry rope.

" Oh, glory be to me!" says he, "an' fame's unfadin'
        flowers,
I ride my good top-hoss to-day and I'm top hand
        of the Lazy-J,
So Kitty-cat, you're ours!"

The lion licked his paws so brown and dreamed soft
        dreams of veal,
As High-Chin's loop come circlin' down and roped
        him round his meal;
He yowled quick fury to the world and all the hills
        yelled back:
That top-hoss give a snort and whirled and Bob
        caught up the slack.

" Oh, glory be to me!" says he, "we'll hit the glory
        trail.
No man has looped a lion's head and lived to drag
        the bugger dead,
Till I shall tell the tale."

'Way high up in the Mokiones that top-hoss done
        his best
'Mid whippin' brush and rattlin' stones from canon-
        floor to crest;
Up and down and round and cross Bob pounded
        weak and wan,
But pride still glued him to his hoss and glory drove
        him on:

" Oh, glory be to me," says he, " this glory trail is
        rough,
I'll keep this dally round the horn until the toot
        of judgment morn,
Before I holler 'nough!"

Three suns had rode their circle home beyond the
    desert rim
And turned their star herds loose to roam the
    ranges high and dim,
And whenever Bob turned and hoped the limp re-
    mains to find,
A red-eyed lion, belly-roped, but healthy, loped
    behind!

"Oh, glory be to me," says Bob, "he kain't be
    drug to death!
These heroes that I've read about were only fools
    that stuck it out
To the end of mortal breath!"

'Way high up in the Mokiones, if you ever come
    there at night,
You'll hear a ruckus amongst the stones that'll
    lift your hair with fright;
You'll see a cow-hoss thunder by and a lion trail
    along,
And the rider bold, with chin on high, sings forth
    his glory song;

"Oh, glory be to me!" says he, "and to my mighty
    noose!
Oh, pardner, tell my friends below I took a ragin'
    dream in tow,
And if I did n't lay him low, — I never turned him
    loose!"

JOHN GARNER'S TRAIL HERD

*Written by one of the waggoners at Fort Worth, Texas,
many years ago. I first heard it sung in the Spearfish
Valley, Dakota.*

Come, all you old-timers, and listen to my song;
I'll make it short as possible and I'll not keep you
        long;
I'll relate to you about the time you all remember
        well
When we with old Joe Garner drove a beef herd up
        the trail.

When we left the ranch it was early in the spring,
We had as good a corporal as ever rope did
        swing;
Good hands and good horses, good outfit through
        and through, —
We went well equipped, we were a jolly crew.

We had no little herd — two thousand head or
        more —
And some as wild brush beeves as you ever saw
        before.
We swung to them all the way and sometimes by
        the tail, —
Oh, you know we had a circus as we all went up the
        trail.

Till we reached the open plains everything went
        well,
And then them cattle turned in and dealt us merry
        hell.

They stampeded every night that came and did it
    without fail, —
Oh, you know we had a circus as we all went up the
    trail.

We would round them up at morning and the boss
    would make a count,
And say, "Look here, old punchers, we are out
    quite an amount;
You must make all losses good and do it without
    fail,
Or you'll never get another job driving up the
    trail."

When we reached Red River we gave the Inspector
    the dodge.
He swore by God Almighty in jail old Joe should
    lodge.
We told him if he'd taken our boss and had him
    locked in jail,
We would shore get his scalp as we all came down
    the trail.

When we reached the Reservation how squirmish
    we did feel,
Although we had tried old Garner and knew him
    true as steel.
And if we would follow him and do as he said to,
That old bald-headed cow-thief would surely take
    us through

When we reached Dodge City we drew our four
    months' pay:
Times was better then, boys, than they are to-day.

The way we drank and gambled a
    around, —
"Say, a crowd of Texas cowboys l
    our town."

The cowboy sees many hardships, al
    them well;
The fun we had upon that trip no
    can tell.
The cowboy's life is a dreary life, th
    it is no load,
And he always spends his money lil
    in the road.

If ever you meet old Garner, you must
    the square,
For he is the biggest cow-thief that e
    out there.
But if you want to hear him roar and s
    tale,
Just ask him about the time we all went

THE JOLLY COWBOY

First heard this sung by Dick Wilson, El Pc
Author unknown.

My lover is a cowboy, he's brave and kind
He rides a Spanish pony, he throws a lass
And when he comes to see me our vows w
    deem,
He throws his arms around me and thus b
    sing:

We bid farewell to the city life,
    we come,
And back to dear old Texas, t
    home."

Oh, he is coming back to mar
    loves;
He says I am his darling, I am
Some day we two will marry and
    roam,
But settle down with Mary in a

"Ho, I'm a jolly cowboy, from
Give me my bond to Mary, I'll
    trail.
I love the rolling prairies, they
    and strife,
But I'll quit the herd of longhorns
    little wife."

THE LAST LONGH

I have been unable to trace the au
Have heard it sung in many places

An ancient long-horned b
Lay dying by the river;
There was lack of vegeta
And the cold winds made
A cowboy sat beside him,
With sadness in his face,
To see his final passing,
This last of a noble race.

The ancient eunuch struggled
And raised his shaking head,
Saying, "I care not to linger
When all my friends are dead.
These Jerseys and these Holsteins,
They are no friends of mine;
They belong to the nobility
Who live across the brine.

"Tell the Durhams and the Herefords
When they come a-grazing round,
And see me lying stark and stiff
Upon the frozen ground,
I don't want them to bellow
When they see that I am dead,
For I was born in Texas,
Near the river that is Red.

"Tell the coyotes, when they come at night,
A-hunting for their prey,
They might as well go further,
For they'll find it will not pay:
If they attempt to eat me
They very soon will see
That my bones and hide are petrified, —
They'll find no beef on me.

"I remember in the seventies,
Full many summers past,
There was grass and water plenty,
But it was too good to last.
I little dreamed what would happen
Some twenty summers hence,

When the nester came with his wife, his kids,
His dogs, and his barbed-wire fence."
His voice sank to a murmur,
His breath was short and quick;
The cowboy tried to skin him
When he saw he could n't kick;
He rubbed his knife upon his boot
Until he made it shine,
But he never skinned old longhorn,
'Caze he could n't cut his rine.

And the cowboy riz up sadly
And mounted his cayuse,
Saying, "The time has come when longhorns
And cowboys are no use."
And while gazing sadly backward
Upon the dead bovine
His bronc stepped in a dog-hole
And fell and broke his spine.

The cowboys and the longhorns
Who pardnered in eighty-four
Have gone to their last round-up
Over on the other shore;
They answered well their purpose,
But their glory must fade and go,
Because men say there's better things
In the modern cattle show.

LAS VEGAS REUNION

By N. Howard Thorp

Written for the annual Las Vegas, New Mexico, Re-union.

Come on, all you cow-punchers,
To the round-up in July,
Where the Busters get together,
En the old broncs go sky-high;
We've got 'em spoiled en tricky,
Outlaws from far en near,
En we've got the boys to fork 'em,
Who know not the word of fear.

The cry of all the cowboys now
Is "To the Meadow City or bust!"
From far Colorado's borders
They come a-spurrin' through the dust.
You don't see prairie-schooners
A-headin' now this way,
But 'mobiles come by thousands
To the Reunion's openin' day!

Cow-girls from far Montana
En the little Prairie Rose,
They can ride 'em slick en keerless
Es everybody knows;
So come on to the Meadow City,
The key's thrown plumb away,
En everybody 's welcome
To the Cowboy's openin' day!

Chorus

With angora chaps en carnival hats,
Checked shirts en handkerchiefs loud,
Come straddle yer horse en ride with us,
Come ride with the Wild West crowd!
Fer we're jest cow-eatin' persons,
There's a welcome fer every one;
So whip up yer horse en lope across
To the Cowboys' Re-un-ion!

"'LIGHT, STRANGER, 'LIGHT"

By N. Howard Thorp

For this is the law of the Western range,
When a stranger hails in sight —
"Jest tie up your hoss in the old corral,
En 'light, stranger, 'light!"

'T is a land of hospitable people,
You're welcome in daytime or night;
Always one more chair at the table,
So it's "'Light, stranger, 'light!"

We don't ask no inquisitive questions,
If your people are native or white;
At our ranch you will find you are welcome,
So it's "'Light, stranger, 'light!"

You may be an outlaw, or preacher,
Got into some place kinda tight —
Some day you'll return the favor,
So it's "'Light, stranger, 'light!"

We are just plain cow-folks in Texas,
But you'll find we are all about right;
You may stay for a year and be welcome,
So it's " 'Light, stranger, 'light!"

LITTLE ADOBE CASA

By Tom Beasley

*Written in the spring of 1887 and sung in the cow-camps
by the author, who had a good voice. While Beasley
was working for me I heard him sing the song. There's
a story about a nugget of gold, Henry Heap (the bank
watchman in El Paso), and Tom Beasley that some of
you old-timers may recall, but I can't write it here.
Remember?*

Just one year ago to-day,
I left my Eastern home,
Hunting for a fortune and for fame.
Little did I think that now
I'd be in Mexico
In this little adobe casa on the plains.

Chorus

*The roof is ocateo,
The coyotes far and near;
The Greaser roams about the place all day;
Centipedes and tarantulas
Crawl o'er me while I sleep
In my little adobe casa on the plains.*

Alacranies on the ceiling,
Cucarachas on the wall,
My bill-of-fare is always just the same;
Frijoles and tortillas

Stirred up in chile sauce
In my little adobe casa on the plains.

But if some dark-eyed mujer
Would consent to be my wife,
I would try to be contented and remain
'Til fate should show a better place
To settle down for life
Than this little adobe casa on the plains.

THE LITTLE COW-GIRL

By N. Howard Thorp

Daddy come from Brownsville,
En Maw from San Antone;
We come here in a wagon
That ud rock en squeak en groan;

We brought our stock en horses;
The Boys come on afore;
En Dad was playin' all the way
"Old Turkey in the Straw"!

There's me en Sister Annie,
En Tom, en Si, en Budd;
We all was raised with cattle,
So I guess it's in our blood;

En I shore love the dances —
Folks say I take after Maw —
When Dad takes down his fiddle
En plays "Turkey in the Straw"!

We ain't jest much on stylish,
But we got a good Home Ranch,
En the little old horse-pasture
Runs clear down to the branch.

En we're all plumb contented
Since Dad put hinges on the door,
En with his old brown fiddle
Plays "Turkey in the Straw"!

I got er pair er shop-made boots
That Dad had made fer me,
Er pair er silver-mounted spurs
Es pretty es can be;

We ride ter all the dances,
En when I get on the floor,
I'm sure to hear Dad playin'
"Old Turkey in the Straw"!

I've got a young cow-puncher roped,
I've got 'im on my string,
En everything is lovely,
We'll be married in the spring;

Es we ain't much on religion,
We'll be married by the Law,
En I kin hear Dad playin'
"Old Turkey in the Straw"!

LITTLE JOE, THE WRANGLER

By N. Howard Thorp

*Written by me on trail of herd of O Cattle from Chimney
Lake, New Mexico, to Higgins, Texas, 1898. On trail
were the following men, all from Sacramento Mountains,
or Crow Flat: Pap Logan, Bill Blevens, Will Brownfield,
Will Fenton, Lije Colfelt, Tom Mews, Frank Jones, and
myself. It was copyrighted and appeared in my first edition of "Songs of the Cowboys," published in 1908.*

Little Joe, the wrangler, will never wrangle more;
    His days with the "remuda" — they are done.
'T was a year ago last April he joined the outfit here,
    A little "Texas stray" and all alone.

'T was long late in the evening he rode up to the herd
    On a little old brown pony he called Chow;
With his brogan shoes and overalls a harder-look-
        ing kid,
    You never in your life had seen before.

His saddle 't was a Southern kack built many years
        ago,
    An O.K. spur on one foot idly hung,
While his "hot roll" in a cotton sack was loosely
        tied behind
    And a canteen from the saddle horn he'd slung.

He said he had to leave his home, his daddy'd
        married twice,
    And his new ma beat him every day or two;
So he saddled up old Chow one night and "lit a
        shuck" this way —
    Thought he'd try and paddle now his own canoe.

Said he'd try and do the best he could if we'd only
    give him work,
  Though he did n't know "straight" up about a
    cow;
So the boss he cut him out a mount and kinder put
    him on,
  For he sorter liked the little stray somehow.

Taught him how to herd the horses and learn to
    know them all,
  To round 'em up by daylight; if he could
To follow the chuck-wagon and to always hitch the
    team
  And help the "cosinero" rustle wood.

We'd driven to Red River and the weather had
    been fine;
  We were camped down on the south side in a bend,
When a norther commenced blowing and we
    doubled up our guards,
  For it took all hands to hold the cattle then.

Little Joe, the wrangler, was called out with the rest,
  And scarcely had the kid got to the herd,
When the cattle they stampeded; like a hailstorm,
    long they flew,
  And all of us were riding for the lead.

'Tween the streaks of lightning we could see a
    horse far out ahead —
  'T was little Joe, the wrangler, in the lead;
He was riding "Old Blue Rocket" with his slicker
    'bove his head,
  Trying to check the leaders in their speed.

At last we got them milling and kinder quieted
    down,
  And the extra guard back to the camp did go;
But one of them was missin', and we all knew at a
    glance
  'T was our little Texas stray — poor Wrangler Joe.

Next morning just at sunup we found where Rocket
    fell,
  Down in a washout twenty feet below;
Beneath his horse, mashed to a pulp, his spurs had
    rung the knell
  For our little Texas stray — poor Wrangler Joe.

LOVE ON THE RANGE

*I got this from Doc Henderson at an Albuquerque Live
Stock Association meeting.*

Little gal, I'm not a singer; if I were I'd sing to you
A tale of love that sure would be a wonder;
It would beat them opry singers when they sing,
    "Love I'll be true —
As true as moon and stars a-shining yonder."

My hands are big, and clumsy — I can't pick the
    light guitar;
And no doubt you'll say my lingo's idle prattle;
But what can you expect? I'm from the Double
    Circle-Bar,
Where all my fingers learned was punching cattle.

I know the trail blindfolded and I never knew a fear,
For I've followed it for years, honeysuckle;

I can shoot and throw a rope and brand a crazy,
    locoed steer —
I can ride a bucking bronc and make him knuckle.

I can quiet restless cattle when the leader's getting
    wild,
And the lightning flash is 'nuff to make you dizzy;
I can soothe 'em like a mother when she's croonin'
    to her child —
But it something makes a man get might busy!

But my song — it's meek and humble; there is
    nothing I can sing
That in any way my sentiments can utter;
Since I saw your flashing eye, your winning smile
    — yes, everything
In your outfit — they have set my heart a-flutter.

So, Chiquita, if you'll let me, I would like to brand
    you mine —
Will you share with me the storms and sunny
    weather?
Ah! Your arms, your lips, Chiquita — they are
    sweeter than old wine!
Come, we'll hit life's trail and follow it — together!

A MAN NAMED HODS

*Heard this first over on the Via Grande, sung by a
puncher named Liston.*

Come, all you old cow-punchers, a story I will tell,
And if you'll all be quiet, I sure will sing it well;
And if you boys don't like it, you can all go to hell.

Back in the day when I was young, I knew a man
    named Hods;
He was n't fit fer nothin' cep turnin' up the clods.

But he came West in fifty-three behind a pair of mules
And 't was hard to tell between the three which
    was the biggest fools.

Up on the plains old Hods he got — there his
    trouble began.
Oh, he sure did get in trouble, — and old Hodsie
    was a man.

He met a bunch of Indian bucks led by Geronimo,
And what them Indians did to him — well, shorely
    I don't know.

But they lifted off old Hodsie's skelp and left him
    out to die,
And if it had n't been for me, he'd been in the
    sweet by and by.

But I packed him to Santa Fé, and there I found his
    mules,
For them dad-blamed two critters had got the In-
    dians fooled.

I don't know how they done it, but they shore did
    get away,
And them two is livin' up to this very day.

Old Hodsie's feet got toughened up; he got to be
    a sport;
He opened up a gamblin' house and a place of low
    resort;

He got the prettiest dancing girls that ever could
    be found, —
Them girls' feet was like rubber balls, they never
    stayed on the ground.

And then thar came Billy the Kid, he envied Hod-
    sie's wealth;
He told old Hods to leave the town, 't would be
    better for his health;
Old Hodsie took the hint and got, but he carried
    all his wealth.

And he went back to Noo York State with lots of
    dinero
And now they say he's senator, but of that I shore
    don't know.

THE MULE-SKINNERS

*Got this song from John Caldwell, at Lake Valley, New
Mexico. He was bronco-buster for S.L.C. outfit.*

In readin' the story of early days, it's a cause of
    much personal pain
At the way the author-men leave out us in charge
    of the wagon train;
Granted the rest of 'em worked and fit in the best
    way that they could do —
If it was n't for us that skinned the mules, how
    would the bunch have come through?

We have frosted ourselves on the prairie sweeps
    a-bringin' the Sioux to book,
And the sojer men never had no kick that the front
    rank had been forsook;

They cussed warm holes in the blizzard's teeth
    when waitin' fer grub and tents,
But the comforts of home we allus brung though
    at times at our expense.

We have sweated and swore in the desert land
    where the white sand glares like snow,
A-rompin' around forty rods from hell playin' tag
    with Geronimo;
We larruped the jacks when the bullets flew and
    then when 't was gettin' too hot,
We used for our breastworks mules, dead mules,
    and we give 'em back shot for shot.

We never was rigged up purty, of course, and we
    did n't talk too perlite,
But we brung up the joltin' wagon train to the trail
    end of every fight;
We made a trail through the hostile lands and our
    whip was the victory's key,
So why in the name of all that's fair can't we figger
    in history?

MUSTANG GRAY

*Authorship credited to Tom Grey, Tularosa, New Mexico.
I first heard it sung by a man named Sanford, who kept
a saloon in La Ascension, Mexico, about 1888.*

There was a brave old Texan,
They called him Mustang Gray;
He left his home when but a youth,
Went ranging far away.

But he'll go no more a-ranging,
The savage to affright;
He has heard his last war-whoop,
And fought his last fight.

He ne'er would sleep within a tent,
No comforts would he know;
But like a brave old Tex-i-can,
A-ranging he would go.

When Texas was invaded
By a mighty tyrant foe,
He mounted his noble war-horse,
And a-ranging he did go.

Once he was taken prisoner,
Bound in chains upon the way;
He wore the yoke of bondage
Through the streets of Monterey.

A señorita loved him,
And followed by his side;
She opened the gates and gave to him
Her father's steed to ride.

God bless the señorita,
The belle of Monterey,
She opened wide the prison door,
And let him ride away.

And when his veteran's life was spent,
It was his last command
To bury him on Texas soil
On the banks of the Rio Grande;

And there the lonely traveler,
When passing by his grave,
Will shed a farewell tear
O'er the bravest of the brave.

And he'll go no more a-ranging,
The savage to affright;
He has heard his last war-whoop,
And fought his last fight.

MY LITTLE BROWN MULE

By N. Howard Thorp

Written in 1912, at Santa Fe, concerning a pet trick mule I owned.

His mammy's a burro, his daddy's a horse;
Of course you'll all think it's a mighty queer cross.
He's got brains in his eyes, he's nary a fool;
As smart as a cricket, my little brown mule.

He's always in mischief, he'll shy at a bug;
When he sees a tin Lizzy he'll jump like a frog;
He's a voice like a trumpet, his coat's always bright;
He's as gentle as can be if the cinch is n't tight.

Just pull on that flank cinch a little too long
And he won't do a thing till you are mounted and on;
Then farewell, relations, good-bye to the crowd,
For you are off on a journey high up in the clouds.

At night I don't stake him, just turn him foot-loose,
And inside of two hours he's as full as a goose;

He's a great old camp-robber when the boys are in
　　bed —
Roots among the bake ovens for bacon and bread.

He's a great one to wrangle on, he knows every
　　horse,
And if one of 'em's missing he's as mad as the
　　boss;
His sense just come natural, he was never in
　　school,
He's as wise as a parson, my little brown mule.

Did you ask if I'd sell him — well, not on your
　　life;
The day we were married I gave him to the wife;
And now two of my kids daily ride him to school;
Oh, no, money can't buy him, my little brown
　　mule.

NEW NATIONAL ANTHEM

Accredited to Burr Sims. Heard it sung at a matador
camp in the Panhandle of Texas.

　　　My country, 't is of thee,
　　　Land where things used to be
　　　So cheap we croak.
　　　Land of the mavericks,
　　　Land of the puncher's tricks,
　　　Thy culture-inroad picks
　　　The hide of this peeler-bloke.

　　　Some of the punchers swear
　　　That what they eat and wear

Takes all their calves.
Others vow that they
Eat only once a day
Jerked beef and prairie hay,
Washed down with tallow salves.

These salty dogs but crave,
To pull them out the grave,
Just one Kiowa spur.
They know they still will dine
On flesh and beef the time;
But give us, Lord divine,
One " hen-fruit stir."

Our father's land, with thee,
Best trails of liberty,
We chose to stop.
We don't exactly like
So soon to henceward hike,
But, hell, we'll take the pike
If this don't stop.

NIGGER "'LASSES": THREE-BLOCK BRONCO-BUSTER

By N. Howard Thorp

He ca-su-ied * wid me, most ruinous,
Till ma haid jest popped de ceilin',
Ma stummick got tangled up wid my feet
Till it done lost all feelin';
Ma old black nose commenced ter bleed,

* Ca-su-ied, southern Texas word for bucking.

Everything went round;
When I waked up in a hour er two,
I was spraddled on de ground!

En I was jest a-hummin', —

> *Oh, dere ain't no horse what can't be rode,*
> *Dat's what de white folks say!*
> *En dere ain't a man what can't be throwed,*
> *OH, MAH!* —
> > *I finds it jest dat way!*

Den dey cotched dat horse too quick to suit,
En brought him back ter me,
En I hobbled my stirrups en wrapped my rowels,
En I hollered, "Turn him free!"
Den he bent en he twisted, en he bowed en he
    moaned,
En done der grand grape-vine;
I waked up a-straddle of er cactus bush,
But dis song I had in mind, —

> *Oh, dere ain't no horse what can't be rode,*
> *Dat's what de white folks say!*
> *En dere ain't a man what can't be throwed,*
> *OH, MAH!* —
> > *I finds it jest dat way!*

Den I grabs dat bronc en I piles aboard,
Says I, "Ole horse, good-bye!
I'se got yo' number sure dis time,
I doan care what yer try!"
Bout den he gimme de ole sun-fish,
Rail-fence, en do-se-do;
En it broke my heart fer us ter part,
But I had ter let him go —

Oh, dere ain't no horse what can't be rode,
Dat's what de white folks say!
En dere ain't a man what can't be throwed,
OH, MAH! —
　　　　I finds it jest dat way!

NIGHT-HERDING SONG

This is part of an old song, slightly changed. I lost the other verses when one of my ranch buildings burned down at Palma, New Mexico, some years ago.

Oh, slow up, dogies, quit your roving round,
You have wandered and tramped all over the ground;
Oh, graze along, dogies, and feed kinda slow,
And don't forever be on the go, —
Oh, move slow, dogies, move slow.

I have circle-herded, trail-herded, night-herded,
　　　　and cross-herded, too,
But to keep you together that's what I can't do;
My horse is leg-weary and I'm awful tired,
But if you get away I'm sure to get fired, —
Bunch up, little dogies, bunch up.

Oh, say, little dogies, when are you goin' to lay down
And quit this forever siftin' around?
My limbs are weary, my seat is sore;
Oh, lay down, dogies, like you've laid before, —
Lay down, little dogies, lay down.

Oh, lay still, dogies, since you have laid down,
Stretch away out on the big open ground;
Snore loud, little dogies, and drown the wild sound
That will all go away when the day rolls round, —
Lay still, little dogies, lay still.

THE OLD CHISHOLM TRAIL

*The origin of this song is unknown. There are several
thousand verses to it — the more whiskey the more
verses. Every puncher knows a few more verses. Sung
from the Canadian line to Mexico.*

Come along, boys, and listen to my tale,
I'll tell you of my trouble on the old Chisholm Trail.

*Coma ti yi youpy, youpy ya, youpy ya,
Coma ti yi youpy, youpy ya.*

I started up the trail October twenty-third,
I started up the trail with the 2-U herd.

Oh, a ten-dollar hoss and a forty-dollar saddle, —
And I'm goin' to punchin' Texas cattle.

I woke up one mornin' afore daylight,
And afore I sleep the moon shines bright.

Old Ben Bolt was a blamed good boss,
But he'd go to see the girls on a sore-backed hoss.

Old Ben Bolt was a fine old man,
And you'd know there was whiskey wherever he'd
land.

My hoss throwed me off at the creek called Mud,
My hoss throwed me off round the 2-U herd.

Last time I saw him he was goin' cross the level
A-kickin' up his heels and a-runnin' like the devil.

It's cloudy in the west, a-lookin' like rain,
And my damned old slicker's in the wagon again.

Crippled my hoss, I don't know how,
Ropin' at the horns of a 2-U cow.

We hit Caldwell and we hit her on the fly,
We bedded down the cattle on the hill close by.

No chaps, no slicker, and it's pourin' down rain,
And I swear, by God, I'll never night-herd again.

Feet in the stirrups and seat in the saddle,
I hung and rattled with them longhorn cattle.

Last night I was on guard and the leader broke the
     ranks,
I hit my horse down the shoulders and I spurred
     him in the flanks.

The wind commenced to blow and the rain began to
     fall,
Hit looked, by grab, like we was goin' to lose 'em
     all.

I jumped in the saddle and grabbed holt the horn,
Best blamed cow-puncher ever was born.

I popped my foot in the stirrup and gave a little yell,
The tail cattle broke and the leaders went to hell.

I don't give a damn if they never do stop;
I'll ride as long as an eight-day clock.

Foot in the stirrup and hand on the horn,
Best damned cowboy ever was born.

I herded and hollered and I done very well,
Till the boss said, "Boys, just let 'em go to hell."

Stray in the herd, and the boss said kill it,
So I shot him in the rump with the handle of the
    skillet.

We rounded 'em up and put 'em on the cars,
And that was the last of the old Two Bars.

Oh, it's bacon and beans 'most every day, —
I'd as soon be eatin' prairie hay.

I'm on my horse and I'm goin' at a run,
I'm the quickest shootin' cowboy that ever pulled
    a gun.

I went to the wagon to get my roll,
To come back to Texas, dad-burn my soul.

I went to the boss to draw my roll,
He had it figgered out I was nine dollars in the hole.

I'll sell my outfit just as soon as I can,
I won't punch cattle for no damned man.

Goin' back to town to draw my money,
Goin' back home to see my honey.

With my knees in the saddle and my seat in the sky,
I'll quit punchin' cows in the sweet by and by.

Coma ti yi youpy, youpy ya, youpy ya,
Coma ti yi youpy, youpy ya.

THE OLD COWMAN

By Scott Levitt, Great Falls, Montana

Got song from Joel Thomas, but at the time I did not know author's name.

When the sap comes up through the cottonwood
    roots,
And the first birds light 'mongst the quaking asp
    shoots;
When the last brown edge at the sprinkling snow
Shows a crocus bloom and the cattle low
To the smell of spring from the greening buttes;
Then my winter of years feels a pulsing flood
And a discontent is let loose in my blood;
For the past comes up like a mist-robed sun,
And the sap of old longings begins to run
Till a thousand wishes burst into bud!
From out the past rides a care-free crew,
Steady and reckless right wild, but true —
Big Sag Bill and old Milk River Blake,
Musselshell Jack and Pecos Jake,
A-riding ahead of 'em two by two!
Now the coyotes call to the round-up camp,
And the night herd's out where the grass grows
    damp;
The herders are singing a soothing tune,
For the cows are restless beneath the moon,
And I hear 'em bawling and hear 'em stamp!
And, oh, what singing from out the night!
Not the voice nor the tune, but a something quite

Filled with trust; and the milling cows
Forget stampeding and start to browse,
For the voice of the herder has set them right.
Give me one more day of the old free land,
Uncursed by a road or a barbed-wire strand;
A horse to ride and the sight, as I pass
Of a thousand horns rising out of the grass,
And I'll push back my chair and lay down my
      hand!
Let me ride, old-timer, ride into the west,
Till I'm lost in the sunset upon the crest —
And with it draw down to whatever lies
On the range that's hid till we top the rise;
Where the round-up boss has staked out what's
      best.
Old Milk River Blake and Big Sag Bill,
And Jack and Jake, at the top o' the hill,
Are waiting to ride like we used to ride
At the round-up camp down the Great Divide,
Till the boss of all herders sings, "Peace, be still."

OL' DYNAMITE

By Phil Le Noir

The outlaw stands with blindfold eyes,
    His feet set wide apart;
His coal-black hide gleams in the sun —
    Thar's killin' in his heart.

A puncher squats upon his heels,
    His saddle at his side;
He's sizin' up Ol' Dynamite,
    That he is booked to ride.

The cowboy rises, lifts his saddle —
  A little tune he's hummin' —
Walks catlike all around the hoss —
  "Hold him, boys, I'm comin'."

Now up above the outlaw's back
  He lifts the load of leather;
Then care-ful-lee he lets it down,
  Like the droppin' of a feather.

Ol' Dynamite he stands stock-still,
  Plumb like a gentled pony.
A leap, a yell! an' Buck 's all set —
  "On with the cer-e-mo-nee."

The snubbers rip the blindfold off,
  The punchers yip and yell;
Ol' Dynamite gives one grand snort,
  Then starts his little hell.

He plunges forward on his feet,
  His hind heels in the air;
Then up and down he bucks and backs
  Like a loco rockin'-chair.

But now he stops — he spins around —
  He bawls, he bites, he kicks!
He r'ars straight up into the air,
  Then down on two steel sticks.

But look! "My Gawd!" The crowd screams out,
  "He's boltin' for the stand!"
Then just as quick he jerks up short —
  An' thar 's Buck a-stickin' grand.

Buck leaps to earth, lifts his hat,
    Bows to the whirl of cheers —
Then turning slides his saddle off,
    An' quickly disappears.

OLD GRAZIN' BEN
By N. Howard Thorp

In seventy-six, or thereabouts, when the Black Hills
    made the strike,
En new camps sprung up like mushrooms in the
    cañons overnight,
'T was the twenty-mule team that made the trip
    from the Hills to Camp Supply,
Or the big ox team with their flanks drawn lean
When the water-holes went dry.

Yer could see 'em for miles a-comin',
As the alkali dust would rise,
Each skinner a handkerchief around his head
Ter kind 'er protect his eyes.
With a " Get up! Tobe, blank, blank, you buck,
I'll skin yer alive, yer dub!"
They'd sweat and strain 'gainst collar and chain
Through 'dobe, sand, and mud.

These were the teams that kept at work
The men who were diggin' the gold,
Workin' at rocker and riffle
In those placer camps of old;
These were the men who made history,
The men who supplied the fuel;
Their bones lie scattered along the trail
Side by side with the ox and the mule.

Bull-whackers, en skinners, en swampers,
The men who handled the teams,
Bringing provisions over the plain,
It's befitting to me, it seems,
That their deeds should be ever remembered
'Mongst the best of the frontiersmen;
So three cheers for one I remember well,
Three cheers for Old Grazin' Ben.

OLD HANK

By N. Howard Thorp

Driftin' along the rim-rock, old Camp-Robber
and I,
Out on a scoutin' trip, circlin' the flat lands
dry,
Cuttin' the sign of the cattle, watchin' which way
they drift,
Pullin' 'em out of the bog-holes, givin' the weak
ones a lift,
Throwin' 'em back on the Home Range, each day
in a different place,
In slickers en leggins of leather, through sand-
storms that blister your face . . .

Boss in the Ranch House rides easy — *his* days of
worry are gone,
For he made his pile in the old Trail days, the days
of the old longhorn.
Yep, I'm only a worn-out old Puncher — though
the Boss thinks a *heap* of me!
For I was with him on the Pecos, in the Raid of
Seventy-Three! . . .

Then he married, en got him religion, en tells how
you must n't do wrong,
How a Brand is the cowman's protection — then
he 'll deal you a Gospel Song!

But I 'll tell you, Old Hank was the slickest, that
ever laid line on a steer,
Or burnt over a brand with a runnin'-iron, or worked
on an old cow's ear!
'Course, friends, all this talk 's confidential, — I
would n't want Old Hank to see
That I have n't changed *my* damned religion, since
the Trail Herd of Seventy-Three!

"OLD NORTH"

By N. Howard Thorp

When the Mormons drifted southward,
He was one of a ten-span team,
The biggest young ox them Utah
Bull-whackers hed ever seen.

Tawny en bony en holler,
At three years full six feet tall,
En he 'd break the chain whenever he 'd
strain
En a heavy wagon stall.

Out of a team of twenty,
Which died in the White Sands Pass,
He alone pulled through en made his way
To the springs of San Nicolas.

Twenty Mormon women,
In all, fifty Mormon souls,
Died from the lack of water,
Paying the desert toll.

The ranchmen, on learning the story,
How every one had died,
Let the big steer have his freedom
Through the Organ Valley wide.

In the winter he'd drift down southward
To the Franklin Mountains warm,
In the summer you'd find him grazin'
On the top of El Torro's horn.

No one ever molests him,
A monument he stands
To those pioneers in search of homes,
That gallant Mormon band.

This was the story as told me
By a ranchman's little lass,
Of "North," the steer who roams the plains,
And of those in the White Sands Pass.

OLD PAINT

*Heard this sung by a puncher who had been on a spree
in Pecos City. He had taken a job temporarily as sheep-
rustler for an outfit in Independence Draw, down the river,
and was ashamed of the job. I won't mention his name.*

Refrain:

*Good-bye, Old Paint, I'm a-leavin' Cheyenne,
Good-bye, Old Paint, I'm a-leavin' Cheyenne.*

My foot in the stirrup, my pony won't stand;
Good-bye, Old Paint, I'm a-leavin' Cheyenne.

I'm a-leavin' Cheyenne, I'm off for Montan';
Good-bye, Old Paint, I'm a-leavin' Cheyenne.

I'm a-ridin' Old Paint, I'm a-leadin' Old Fan;
Good-bye, Old Paint, I'm a-leavin' Cheyenne.

With my feet in the stirrups, my bridle in my hand;
Good-bye, Old Paint, I'm a-leavin' Cheyenne.

Old Paint's a good pony, he paces when he can;
Good-bye, little Annie, I'm off for Cheyenne.

Oh hitch up your horses and feed 'em some hay,
And seat yourself by me so long as you stay.

My horses ain't hungry, they'll not eat your hay;
My wagon is loaded and rolling away.

My foot in my stirrup, my reins in my hand;
Good-morning, young lady, my horses won't stand.

Good-bye, Old Paint, I'm a-leavin' Cheyenne,
Good-bye, Old Paint, I'm a-leavin' Cheyenne.

OLD PAINT

By N. Howard Thorp

Every time I see an old paint horse, I think of you,
Old paint horse of mine that used to be,
Old pal o' mine that was, the best horse of all,
    because —
That's why, old horse, at last I set you free!

I've bought 'em by the thousand, I've owned 'em
　　everywhere —
There's one stands out among 'em all alone;
Paint-marked everywhere, tail a little short o'
　　hair,
Old horse, you never failed to bring me home!

'Member when they stole you from Pass City,
En locked you up inside the Juarez jail?
Said that you had eaten up an *entire* crop of wheat,
En I had to rustle round en get your bail?

En I got you cross the river en matched you in a
　　race,
En we bet the last red dollar we could scrape? —
En how you bit old Rocking Chair, the horse you
　　run against,
En made him turn his head en lose the race?

We was both young en foolish in them green days
　　long ago,
I don't believe in telling stories out of school! —
'Member when we roped the pianner en jerked her
　　out the door?
Hush up! Old Paint! you're talkin' like a fool!

Well, old horse, you're buried, en your troubles,
　　they are done,
But I often sit en think of what we did,
En recall the many scrapes we had, en used to think
　　it fun,
Es we rode along the Rio Grande . . .
　　　　　　　　　　　　Good-bye, old Kid!

OLD-TIME COWBOY

Understand this was written by an old cow-puncher who claims he was dragging his rope along and some one else's calf got tangled up in it, and he landed in the Huntsville Pen. His name was Rogers. I first heard it sung by Tom Beasley, at Hueco Tanks, Texas.

Come, all you melancholy folks, wherever you may be,
I'll sing you about the cowboy whose life is light
    and free;
He roams about the prairie, and at night when he
    lies down,
His heart is as gay as the flowers in May in his bed
    upon the ground.

They're a little bit rough, I must confess, the most
    of them at least;
But if you do not hunt a quarrel, you can live with
    them in peace;
For if you do, you're sure to rue the day you joined
    their band.
They will follow you up and shoot it out with you,
    just man to man.

Did you ever go to a cowboy whenever hungry and dry,
Asking for a dollar and have him you deny?
He'll just pull out his pocket-book and hand you
    a note, —
They are the fellows to help you whenever you are
    broke.

Go to their ranches and stay a while — they never
    ask a cent;
And when they go to town their money is freely spent.

They walk straight up and take a drink, paying for
    every one,
And they never ask your pardon for anything they've
    done.

When they go to their dances, some dance while
    others pat;
They ride their bucking broncos and wear their
    broad-brimmed hats;
With their California saddles and their pants stuck
    in their boots,
You can hear their spurs a-jingling and perhaps
    some of them shoots.

Come, all soft-hearted tenderfeet, if you want to
    have some fun,
Go live among the cowboys, they'll show you how
    it's done;
They'll treat you like a prince, my boys, about them
    there's nothing mean;
But don't try to give them too much advice, for all
    of them ain't green.

"OLD TROUBLE" A L RANCH COLORED COOK

By N. Howard Thorp

Morn's breakin' over de ole Ranch before de moon's
    gone way,
Dat's a sign er early frostin' in de fall;
Two Roosters on de water-trough 'fore de break er
    day, —
Dat's gwine ter make some trouble fer us all.

I see de fethers in ole turkey's tail, all turned en
  pointin' west,
En I see a crippled dog down in de lane;
De sittin' hens 'bout twelve o'clock has all done
  quit de nests, —
Dey's gwine ter be some trouble soon again.

De bees is buzzin' awful loud down in de gums ter-
  day;
Dat ole houn' dog ain't never moved sense noon;
Believe me, Marster Robert, de signs es pointin'
  right,
Dat der's gwine ter be some trouble mighty soon.

I see dat front door open when der warn't no one
  about,
Der smoke blow back from de chimbley in de room,
En I sees dat rockin'-chair commence ter rock
  alone —
Yes, dere's gwine ter be some trouble mighty soon.

ON THE DODGE

By N. Howard Thorp

Well, old horse, you've brought me 'cross the line,
There's a sheriff's posse ridin' close behind,
  But they'll not cross the Boca Grande,
  The Ru-ra-les are too handy,
And here's one Gringo that they'll never find.

Chorus

I don't see why they can't leave me alone,
I'd love to be back in my happy home!

Every time I steal a horse,
Some one raises hell, of course,
Seems I'm always driftin' west from San Antone!

Last week I found a stake-pin I had lost,
Jest an iron one — 'bout a dollar it had cost, —
    On it was tied a rope,
    En it almost got my goat,
When I found the other end tied to a horse!

I'm as innocent as any man can be,
But I'm afraid the Judge will not agree,
    As there is n't any use
    In dishin' up a poor excuse,
I might as well jest saddle up and flee!

THE OVERLAND STAGE

By N. Howard Thorp

They don't drive the Overland Stage no more
Like they used to when I was young,
With four half-broke broncs out in the lead,
En two in the wagon tongue.
With old Dick Huber up on the box,
The messenger by his side,
They'd drive like hell when they heard the yell
Of Apaches on the ride.

The thorough-braces swinging to and fro,
Es we'd hit the chuck-holes deep,
The clatter of chains 'gainst single trees
On the down grade rough and steep;

Es we'd take the hill across the draw,
You'd hear the buckskin pop —
And Huber pullin' on the lines
Es the team would near the top.

What to do in the case of a hold-up
Was all the talk one day.
Jim Black said he'd fork over,
If let go on his way;
Tom Moore 'lowed he'd come a-shootin'
If they tried that game on him,
For he'd been held up once before
On the road to Silver Inn.

The woman passenger we'd picked up,
In the valley at early dawn
Had never moved or spoke a word
Till we'd passed through Hollow Horn.
En I could see quite quick en pronto
That she was bridle-wise;
Though made up of smiles and dimples,
She had the Devil in her eyes.

For her shawl was worn Spanish-wise,
En her eyes alone shone bright,
En seemed to notice yer every move
Es they'd shift from left to right.
En her little slim girlish figure
Seemed pitifully alone,
En made one feel you should always protect
The young away from home.

'Bout then the coach give an awful lurch,
Es we struck the river sand,
When I come to, there stood the girl
With a Winchester in her hand;
"You gents pile out, yer hands hold high!"
Was the order that she gave,
"Just one false play er a crooked move,
En you'll fill an early grave!"

Well, she cleaned us out to the last red cent,
En the messenger, too, er course,
En she made old Huber cut loose the team
En saddle her up a horse.
Es she rode away, we heard her say,
In a voice with a musical note,
"Boys, times have changed on the open range,
Since the women have got the vote!"

THE PECOS RIVER QUEEN

By N. Howard Thorp

*Written on Lower Pecos, New Mexico, June, 1901, after
Roy Bean had told me of this fact concerning Patty.
Copyrighted in my book published in 1908.*

Where the Pecos River winds and turns in its jour-
ney to the sea,
From its white walls of sand and rock striving ever
to be free,
Near the highest railroad bridge that all these mod-
ern times have seen
Dwells fair young Patty Moorhead, the Pecos River
Queen.

She's known by all the cowboys on the Pecos River
    wide;
They know full well that she can shoot, that she can
    rope and ride;
She goes to every round-up, every cow-work with-
    out fail,
Looking out for all her cattle branded "walking
    hog on rail."

She made her start in cattle, yes, made it with her
    rope;
Can tie down e'ry maverick 'fore it can strike a
    lope;
She can rope and tie and brand it as quick as any
    man;
She's voted by all cowboys an A1 top cow-hand.

Across the Comstock railroad bridge, the highest in
    the West,
Patty rode her horse one day a lover's heart to
    test;
For he told her he would gladly risk all dangers
    for her sake,
But the puncher would n't follow, so she's still
    without a mate.

PECOS TOM

By N. Howard Thorp

Where the old Fort Sumner Barracks look down on
    the Pecos wide,
In a dugout near the crossin' we was a-sittin' side
    by side;

Old Pecos Tom, the cowman, en your humble
    servant, me,
Was a-swappin' cow-camp stories in the fall of
    eighty-three.
When my gaze it sort er fastened on a gun slung on
    his side,
Worth some fifteen thousand dollars — say, maybe
    you think I've lied?
But the handle was plumb covered with diamonds
    of all size,
En she'd glitter, en she'd glisten, es she hung down
    from his side.

You could have bought his whole darned outfit fer
    a yearlin' steer er two,
Hat, boots, overalls, en chaps — there was nothin'
    that was new;
Lived down in a dugout, on jest sour-dough bread
    en beef,
En was just about as happy es a Choctaw Indian chief.

Figured he had ten thousand cattle, en the whole
    wide range was his,
En if he wanted a good six-shooter it was no one
    else's biz;
So when he shipped with er train er steers to Chi-
    cago late one fall,
En was strollin' on up State Street, he thought he'd
    make a call

On the biggest jewelry outfit that kept gaudy
    things to wear,
But when he asked fer a six-shooter the Jew clerk
    began to stare;

" Yes, we've got one that was ordered for a bloomin'
    English lord,
But I reckon from your outfit it's a gun you can't
    afford.

" It will cost you fifteen thousand —" Says Old Tom,
    " Just give her here,
You counter-jumpin' gorriff!" — en he grabbed
    him by the ear,
En he peeled off fifteen thousand to the Hebrew
    standin' there,
Sayin', " Don't judge Western cowmen by the out-
    fits that they wear!"

A PRAIRIE SONG

*I heard this sung by a cow-girl at Cheyenne Round-up —
a Miss Windsor.*

Oh, music springs under the galloping hoofs,
    Out on the plains;
Where mile after mile drops behind with a smile,
And to-morrow seems always to tempt and be-
    guile, —
    Out on the plains.

Oh, where are the traces of yesterday's ride?
    There to the north;
Where alfalfa and sage sigh themselves into
    sleep,
Where the buttes loom up suddenly, startling and
    steep, —
    There to the north.

Oh, rest not my pony, there's youth in my heart,
          Out on the plains;
And the wind sings a wild song to rob me of care,
And there's room here to live and to love and to
     dare, —
          Out on the plains.

THE PROSPECTOR

By N. Howard Thorp

*Written at the Slash S W Ranch, on the door of the old
ranch house, in the San Andreas Mountains.*

Twelve years have I lived in this desolate place,
Far from all habitation — not even a face
Have I seen, save Apaches, those unwelcome guests,
Pass me by as I work with my pick in the breast.

Am I one of the millions whose brain-string has
          snapped,
Who sees visions of gold in those canyons un-
          mapped,
Unexplored, unprospected, that lay just ahead,
Near the Arc of the Bow where so many lie dead?

Like all miners I've visions, which may some day
          come true,
Of where I would go and what I would do —
If I'd but once find the vein which carries the ore,
My days of hard work would forever be o'er.

There's a frenzy of fury that boils in one's veins —
Will it pay for the hardships, will it pay for my pains?
'T is a distorted finger that beckons, it seems,
To the land of illusions, the place of my dreams.

PUNCHIN' DOUGH

By Henry Herbert Knibbs

Come, all you young waddies, I'll sing you a song:
Stand back from the wagon — stay where you be-
        long;
I've heard you observin' I'm fussy and slow,
While you're punchin' cattle and I'm punchin'
        dough.

Now I reckon your stomach would grow to your back,
If it wa'n't for the cook that keeps fillin' the slack:
With the beans in the box and the pork in the tub,
I'm a wonderin', now, who would fill you with
        grub?

You think you're right handy with gun and with
        rope,
But I've noticed you're bashful when usin' the soap:
When you're rollin' your Bull for your brown
        cigarette,
I been rollin' dough for the biscuits you et.

When you're cuttin' stock, then I'm cuttin' steak:
When you're wranglin' horses, I'm wranglin' cake:
When you're hazin' the dogies and battin' your
        eyes,
I'm hazin' dried apples that aim to be pies.

You brag about shootin' up windows and lights,
But try shooting biscuits for twelve appetites:
When you crawl from your roll and the ground it is
        froze,
Then who biles the coffee that thaws out your nose?

In the old days the punchers took just what they
    got:
It was sowbelly, beans, and the old coffee-pot;
But now you come howlin' for pie and for cake,
Then you cuss at the cook for a good bellyache.

You say that I'm old, with my feet on the skids;
Well, I'm tellin' you now that you're nothin' but
    kids:
If you reckon your mounts are some snaky and
    raw,
Just try ridin' herd on a stove that won't draw.

When you look at my apron, you're readin' my
    brand,
Four X, which is sign for the best in the land;
On bottle or sack it sure stands for good luck,
So — line up, you waddies, and wrangle your chuck.

No use of your snortin' and fightin' your head:
If you like it with chile, just eat what I said;
For I aim to be boss of this end of the show,
While you're punchin' cattle and I'm punchin'
    dough.

THE RAILROAD CORRAL

*Author unknown. Mailed to me by a friend at Colorado
City, Texas.*

Oh, we're up in the morning ere breaking of the
    day,
The chuck-wagon's busy, the flapjacks in play;

The herd is astir o'er hillside and vale,
With the night riders rounding them into the trail.
Oh, come take up your cinches, come shake out
     your reins;
Come wake your old bronco and break for the
     plains;
Come roust out your steers from the long chaparral,
For the outfit is off to the railroad corral.

The sun circles upward; the steers as they plod
Are pounding to powder the hot prairie sod;
And it seems, as the dust makes you dizzy and sick,
That we'll never reach noon and the cool shady
     creek.
But tie up your kerchief and ply up your nag;
Come dry up your grumbles and try not to lag;
Come with your steers from the long chaparral,
For we're far on the road to the railroad corral.

The afternoon shadows are starting to lean,
When the chuck-wagon sticks in the marshy ravine;
The herd scatters farther than vision can look,
For you can bet all true punchers will help out the
     cook.
Come shake out your rawhide and snake it up fair;
Come break your old bronco to take in his share;
Come from your steers in the long chaparral,
For 't is all in the drive to the railroad corral.

But the longest of days must reach evening at last,
The hills all climbed, the creeks all past;
The tired herd droops in the yellowing light;
Let them loaf if they will, for the railroad's in sight.

So flap up your holster and snap up your belt,
And strap up your saddle whose lap you have felt;
Good-bye to the steers from long chaparral,
For there's a town that's a trunk by the railroad
 corral.

THE RAMBLING COWBOY

*Author supposed to have been K. Tolliver. I first heard
it at Van Horn, Texas.*

There was a rich old rancher who lived in the country by;
He had a lovely daughter on whom I cast my eye;
She was pretty, tall, and handsome, both neat and
 very fair;
There's no other girl in the country with her I
 could compare.

I asked her if she would be willing for me to cross
 the plains;
She said she would be truthful until I returned
 again;
She said she would be faithful until death did prove
 unkind,
So we kissed, shook hands, and parted, and I left
 my girl behind.

I left the state of Texas, for Arizona I was bound;
I landed in Tombstone City, I viewed the place all
 round.
Money and work were plentiful, and the cowboys
 they were kind,
But the only thought of my heart was the girl I left
 behind.

One day, as I was riding across the public square,
The mail-coach came in and I met the driver there;
He handed me a letter which gave me to understand
That the girl I left in Texas had married another
    man.

I turned myself all roundabout, not knowing what
    to do,
But I read on down some further and it proved the
    words were true.
Hard work I have laid over, it's gambling I have
    designed.
I'll ramble this wide world over for the girl I left
    behind.

Come, all you reckless and rambling boys, who
    have listened to this song,
If it has n't done you any good, it has n't done you
    any wrong;
But when you court a pretty girl, just marry her
    while you can,
For if you go across the plains she'll marry another
    man.

SAM BASS

By John Denton, Gainsville, Texas, 1879

*This is the most authentic report on authorship I have re-
ceived. I first heard the song sung in Sidney, Nebraska,
at a dance hall, in 1888.*

Sam Bass was born in Indiana, it was his native
    home,
And at the age of seventeen young Sam began to
    roam.

Sam first came out to Texas a cowboy for to be, —
A kinder-hearted fellow you seldom ever see.

Sam used to deal in race-stock, one called the
Denton mare;
He matched her in scrub races and took her to the
fair.
Sam used to coin the money, and spent it just as
free;
He always drank good whiskey wherever he might
be.

Sam left the Collins ranch, in the merry month of
May,
With a herd of Texas cattle the Black Hills for to
see;
Sold out in Custer City, and then got on a spree, —
A harder set of cowboys you seldom ever see.

On their way back to Texas they robbed the U.P.
train,
And then split up in couples and started out again;
Joe Collins and his partner were overtaken soon,
With all their hard-earned money they had to meet
their doom.

Sam made it back to Texas, all right up with care;
Rode into town of Denton with all his friends to
share.
Sam's life was short in Texas; three robberies did
he do;
He robbed all the passenger mail and express cars
too.

Sam had four companions — four bold and daring
    lads —
They were Richardson, Jackson, Joe Collins, and
    Old Dad;
Four more bold and daring cowboys the Rangers
    never knew,
They whipped the Texas Rangers and ran the boys
    in blue.

Sam and another companion, called Arkansas for
    short,
Was shot by a Texas Ranger by the name of
    Thomas Floyd;
Oh, Tom is a big six-footer and thinks he's mighty
    fly,
But I can tell you his racket, — he's a deadbeat on
    the sly.

Jim Murphy was arrested and then released on bail;
He jumped his bond at Tyler and then took the
    train for Terrell;
But Mayor Jones had posted Jim and that was all a
    stall,
'T was only a plan to capture Sam before the coming
    fall.

Sam met his fate at Round Rock, July the twenty-
    first;
They pierced poor Sam with rifle balls and emptied
    out his purse.
Poor Sam he is a corpse and six foot under clay,
And Jackson in the bushes trying to get away.

Jim had borrowed Sam's good gold and did n't want
    to pay,
The only shot he saw was to give poor Sam away.
He sold out Sam and Barnes and left their friends
    to mourn, —
Oh, what a scorching Jim will get when Gabriel
    blows his horn.

And so he sold out Sam and Barnes and left their
    friends to mourn, —
Oh, what a scorching Jim will get when Gabriel
    blows his horn.
Perhaps he 's got to heaven, there 's none of us can
    say,
But if I am right in my surmise he 's gone the other
    way.

SKY-HIGH

By N. Howard Thorp

The scream of the outlaw split the air
As we tied him hard and fast
To the snubbing-post in the horse corral,
For his turn had come at last

To learn the feel of spurs of steel
As they graze along each side, —
En Bugger pulled up his chaps a hole,
For he was the next to ride.

We knew he 'd strike, we knew he 'd bite,
We knew he 'd kick and rear,
So we grabbed his ears en held his head,
Till Bugger got up near.

He stepped into the saddle
En hollered — "Let 'im go!"
We jerked the blinder from his eyes,
Then stopped to watch the show.

You've all heard of pitchin' horses
From Steamboat down the line,
Old Barometer, en Step Fast,
En a mare they called Divine.

Old Prickly Pear, en Pizen,
Lop Ears, en Stingaree, —
They all wuz Shetland ponies
'Side this horse from Santa Fe.

We asked Red in tones solicitous
If he had made his will,
Had he any girl in Texas
Who really loved him still?

Was there any parting message
That he would like to send,
To some one in his old, old home
Who still might be his friend?

Who was his pet undertaker?
What parson should we get?
Would he have flowers on his coffin?
I can hear old Bugger yet;

"Mosey, you four-flush punchers,
Don't weep no tears for me,
I'm a ridin' kid from Texas,
From the old 3 Bar C!

"Go up, you old Cloud-Getter,
I can see the Pearly Gate,
We're a-doin' the Grand Ascension,
Loopin' the loops, as sure as fate;

"If I'm a judge of horses,
You're not one, two, three,
With the gentle stock we used to ride
At the old 3-C!"

He whipped old Sky-High till he quit,
He roweled him up and down;
Old Sky-High had a plenty,
He could hardly turn around.

En we heard old Bugger hummin',
Es he turned the outlaw free,
"I'm a ridin' kid from Texas,
From the old 3-C!"

A SONG OF THE RANGE

By James Barton Adams

Sent me by Miss Nell Benson

The bawl of a steer to a cowboy's ear is music of
    sweetest strain,
And the yelling notes of the gray coyotes to him are
    a glad refrain;
The rapid beat of his bronco's feet on the sod as he
    speeds along
Keeps 'livening time to the ringing rhyme of his
    rollicking cowboy song.

His eyes are bright and his heart is light as the
    smoke of his cigarette,
There's never a care for his soul to bear, no
    troubles to make him fret;
For a kingly crown in the noisy town his saddle he
    would not change —
No life so free as the life we see 'way out on the
    cattle range.

      Hi-lo! Hi-lay!
     To the range away,
   On the deck of a bronc of steel,
     With a careless flirt
     Of a rawhide quirt
   And a dig of the roweled heel.
     The winds may howl,
    And the thunder growl,
  Or the breeze may softly moan;
     The rider's life
     Is the life for me,
  The saddle a kingly throne.

At the long day's close he his bronco throws with
    the bunch in the hoss corral,
And a light he spies in the bright blue eyes of his
    welcoming rancher gal;
'T is a light that tells of the love that dwells in the
    soul of his little dear,
And a kiss he slips to her waiting lips when no one
    is watching near.
His glad thoughts stray to the coming day when
    away to the town they'll ride,
And the nuptial brand by the parson's hand will be
    placed on his bonnie bride,

And they'll gallop back to the old home shack in the
life that is new and strange —
The rider bold and the girl of gold, the queen of the
cattle range.

Hi-lo! Hi-lay!
For the work is play
When love's in the cowboy's eyes,
When his heart is light
As the clouds of white
That swim in the summer skies;
And his jolly song
Speeds the hours along
As he thinks of the little gal
With the golden hair
Who'll be waiting there
At the gate of the home corral.

SPECKLES

By N. Howard Thorp

This song was written in 1906 at Palma, New Mexico,
my old ranch. I gave the contract to print my first little
book, entitled "Songs of the Cowboys," to Mr. P. A.
Speckman, News Print Shop, Estancia, New Mexico, who
printed it in 1908.

He was little en peaked en thin, en narry a no-
account horse —
Least that's the way you'd describe him in case
that the beast had been lost —
But for single and double cussedness en double
center-fired sin
The horse never come out o' Texas that was half-
way knee-high to him.

The first time that ever I saw him was nineteen
    year ago last spring.
'T was the year we had grasshoppers, that come en
    et up everything,
That a feller rode up here one evening en wanted to
    pen overnight
A small bunch of horses, he said, en I told him I
    guessed 't was all right.

Well, the feller was busted, the horses was thin,
    en the grass around here kind o' good,
En he said if I'd let him hold here a few days, he'd
    settle with me when he could.
So I told him all right, turn them loose down the
    draw, that the latchstring was always un-
    tied;
He was welcome to stop a few days if he liked en
    rest from his long, weary ride.

Well, the cuss stay'd around for two or three weeks
    till at last he decided to go,
And that horse over yonder being too poor to move
    he gimme — the cuss had no dough;
Well, at first the darn brute was as wild as a deer,
    en would snort when he came to the branch,
En it took two cow-punchers, on good horses, too,
    to handle him here at the ranch.

Well, winter come on and the range it got hard, and
    my mustang commenced to get thin,
So I fed him along and rode him around some and
    found out old Speckles was game;
For that was what the other cuss called him, just
    Speckles, no more or no less:

His color, could n't describe it, something like a
    paint-shop in distress.

Them was Indian times, young feller, that I'm
    a-telling about,
And oft's the time I've seen the red men fight and
    put the boys in blue to rout.
A good horse in them days, young feller, would
    often save your life —
One that in any race could hold the pace when the
    red-skin bands were rife.

I was a-settin' one night at sunset, jest inside that
    hall,
En Mollie hed gone to the milk-pen as she heard
    the milk cows bawl,
When out o' brush en thicket, ridin' towards me
    out o' the west,
Comes Antelope John, his horse on the run, en
    ridin' like one possessed.

"Apaches are out!" he shouted; "for God's sake,
    hurry and go!
They're close behind, comin' like the wind; catch
    your horse and come on, Joe!"
Old Speckles was saddled, I grabbed my gun,
    picked Mollie up as I passed;
With the grit of her kind she hung on behind and
    never a question asked.

Down through cañons deep, over mesas steep, Old
    Speckles never failed;
In his heart of steel he seemed to feel the red-skins
    on our trail;

On, ever onward, towards Fort Craig he sped the
　　whole night through;
Though handicapped by a double load, he out-
　　stripped the red-skins too.

Never will I forget that ride, en how at first day-
　　break
We galloped out of the chaparral en entered the old
　　fort gate.

TEN THOUSAND TEXAS RANGERS
By Alice Corbin

*Written in March, 1917, at the time when Germany pro-
posed to Mexico that they retake the "lost provinces" of
Texas, New Mexico, Arizona, and California.*

Ten thousand Texas Rangers are laughin' fit to
　　kill
At the joke of the German Kaiser, an' his fierce,
　　imperious will —
For he sez, sez he, to the Mexican boob, hidin'
　　behind his beard,
"Old Uncle Sam is an easy mark, or so I've always
　　heerd —

"Go up and take his cattle, and take a state or
　　two, —
Texas, New Mexico, Arizone — don't stop before
　　you're through;
For we shall make war together, and together make
　　peace," he said,
Now ain't it a joke — so easy-like — as easy as
　　makin' bread!

Now if he had wanted a gun-man, he could n't
    have chose a worse,
For Pancho Villa has got more knack in fixin' a man
    for the hearse,
And if he had thought that a gun-man could swipe
    that piece of earth,
He should 'a' remembered *we* got the trick of
    handlin' a gun from birth!

Ten thousand Texas Rangers are shakin' with
    wicked glee
At the joke of the German Kaiser in his fierce per-
    plexity;
They are bustin' their buttins with laughin', they
    are laughin' fit to kill —
"By Gawd," sez they, "but that's one on him, by
    Gawd, but that's one on Bill!"

THE TENDERFOOT

By Yank Hitson, Denver, Colorado, 1889

*I got the song from old Battle Axe, whom lots of old
punchers remember, at Phœnix, Arizona, 1899.*

    I thought one spring, just for fun,
    I'd see how cow-punching was done;
    And when the round-ups had begun
    I tackled the cattle-king.
    Says he, "My foreman is in town,
    He's at the plaza, his name is Brown;
    If you'll see him he'll take you down."
    Says I, "That's just the thing."

We started for the ranch next day;
Brown augured me most all the way.
He said that cow-punching was child play,
That it was no work at all, —
That all you had to do was ride,
'T was only drifting with the tide;
Oh, how that old cow-puncher lied —
He certainly had his gall.

He put me in charge of a cavyard,
And told me not to work too hard,
That all I had to do was guard
The horses from getting away;
I had one hundred and sixty head,
I sometimes wished that I was dead;
When one got away, Brown's head turned red,
And there was hell to pay.

Straight to the bushes they would take,
As if they were running for a stake, —
I've often wished their neck they 'd break,
But they would never fall.
Sometimes I could not head them at all,
Sometimes my horse would catch a fall,
And I'd shoot on like a cannon ball
Till the earth came in my way.

They saddled me up an old gray hack
With two set-fasts on his back;
They padded him down with a gunny sack
And used my bedding all.
When I got on he quit the ground,
Went up in the air and turned around,
And I came down and hit the ground, —
It was an awful fall.

They picked me up and carried me in
And rubbed me down with an old stake-pin.
" That's the way they all begin;
You're doing well," says Brown.
" And in the morning, if you don't die,
I'll give you another horse to try."
" Oh, say, can't I walk?" says I.
Says he, " Yes — back to town."

I've traveled up and I've traveled down,
I've traveled this country round and round,
I've lived in city and I've lived in town,
But I've got this much to say:
Before you try cow-punching, kiss your wife,
Take a heavy insurance on your life,
Then cut your throat with a barlow knife, —
For it 's easier done that way.

THE TEXAS COWBOY

*An old song, credited to Al Pease of Round Rock, Texas.
I first heard it sung by J. Latham at La Luz, New Mexico.*

Oh, I am a Texas cowboy,
Far away from home;
If ever I get back to Texas
I never more will roam.

Montana is too cold for me
And the winters are too long;
Before the round-ups do begin,
Our money is all gone.

Take this old hen-skin bedding,
Too thin to keep me warm;
I nearly freeze to death, my boys,
Whenever there's a storm.

And take this old "tarpoleon"
Too thin to shield my frame —
I got it down in New Mexico
A-dealin' a Monte game.

Now to win these fancy leggins
I'll have enough to do;
They cost me twenty dollars
The day that they were new.

I have an outfit on the Musselshell,
But that I'll never see,
Unless I get sent to represent
The circle or D.T.

I've worked up in Nebraska
Where the grass grows ten feet high,
And the cattle are such rustlers
That they seldom ever die;

I've worked up in the sand hills,
And down upon the Platte,
Where the cowboys are good fellows
And the cattle always fat;

I've traveled lots of country, —
Nebraska's hills of sand,
Down through the Indian Nation,
And up the Rio Grande; —

But the Bad lands of Montana
Are the worst I've ever seen,
The cowboys are all tenderfeet,
And the dogies are all lean.

If you want to see some bad lands,
Go over on the Dry;
You will bog down in the coulees
Where the mountains reach the sky.

A tenderfoot to lead you
Who never knows the way;
You are playing in the best of luck
If you eat more than once a day.

Your grub is bread and bacon,
And coffee black as ink;
The water so full of alkali
It is hardly fit to drink.

They will wake you in the morning,
Before the break of day,
And send you on a circle
A hundred miles away.

All along the Yellowstone
'T is cold the year around;
You will surely get consumption
By sleeping on the ground.

Work in Montana
Is six months in the year;
When all your bills are settled,
There is nothing left for beer.

Work down in Texas
Is all the year around;
You will never get consumption
By sleeping on the ground.

Come, all you Texas cowboys,
And warning take from me,
And do not go to Montana
To spend your money free.

But stay at home in Texas,
Where work lasts the year around;
And you will never catch consumption
By sleeping on the ground.

THANKSGIVING ON THE RANCH

By James Barton Adams, Denver

We was settin' 'round the ranch house on the last
    Thanksgivin' Day,
Tellin' yarns an' swappin' fables fer to pass the
    time away;
Fer the owner was religious an' had made it mani-
    fest
That there would n't be no ridin' on a day o' joyful
    rest;
An' we got in a discussion an' a heap o' talk was
    spent
Pro an' con an' vivy vocy what Thanksgivin' reely
    meant;
An' I'll bet a workin' saddle 'gainst a pa'r o' hoss's
    shoes
That there never was another sich a scatterin' o'
    views.

Texas Tony thought 't was taught him when he
    went to Sunday school,
In the days when he was swimmin' in the Baptis'
    pious pool,
That it was a celebration that was started on the
    dock
When the Scribes an' Pharisees was landed onto
    Plymouth Rock.
Bronco Billy said he reckoned Tex had got his
    stories mixed,
That his mem'ry wheels had run too long without
    a-bein' fixed;
That the day, if he remembered, was a day o'
    jubilee
In remembrance of Abe Lincoln settin' all the nig-
    gers free.

Brocky Jim, from Arizony, begged to differ, sayin'
    he
In his younger days had wasted lots o' time on his-
    tory;
An' the day was celebrated in thanksgivin' fer
    the change
When the Revolution fellers drifted off King
    George's range.
Lengthy Jones an' Watt McGovern an' the Rio
    Grandy Kid
Coincided in believin', as the present writer
    did,
It was jest a yearly epock to remind us o' the
    day
When Columbus happened on us in a onexpected
    way.

Uncle Dick, the ol' hoss 'rangler, sot an' smoked
    his pipe till all
O' the fellers with the question then at stake had
    tuk a fall,
An' when asked fer his opinion o' the matter said
    that he
Had his idee o' the objeck o' the yearly jubilee:
'T was a day when all the fellers so inclined could
    show their thanks
Fer whatever they'd a mind to by a-fillin' up their
    tanks
Till their legs got weak an' weary from a-carryin'
    the load —
He had spent the day in Denver an' he reckoned
    that he knowed.

THREE-BLOCK TOM

By N. Howard Thorp

We was trailin' some stolen cattle
In the winter of '98,
From the Sierra Capitanes
Past Dry Red Lake.

On north to the Gran Quivira,
Past the Malapais,
Hugging their trail like leeches
Rode Three-Block Tom and I.

They passed Punta de Agua,
Left Manzanas on the west,
Estancia to the eastward —
They hardly stopped to rest.

Here en there we found a calf
That had played out en dropped behind —
They were making thirty miles a day,
Driving like the wind.

We caught up with them at Cerillos,
On the T.P. Road;
Driv' 'em plain out of the country,
Expecting there to load.

But somehow the rustlers got wind of us,
En quit the cattle there,
En though we hunted for several days
We could n't find the pair.

At last we got instructions
From the supreme boss,
To ship to Kansas City
To Clay, Robinson & Ross.

But when I commenced a-loadin',
I found Tom was n't there;
A puncher told me he was in Lamy,
Loaded up fer fair.

So I hired the two-horse wagon
En set out that night —
When I found Old Tom in Lamy,
He was sure some sight.

He had centipedes and rattlers,
Gila monsters by the score,
Puttin' them through their paces
On Jon Pflueger's barroom floor.

Well, at last I got him headed
Fer the loadin' pens,
En right there, friend neighbors,
When my trouble it began.

For he would n't make a wiggle
Till I'd bought a few drinks more;
With his jug hugged up tight in his arms
I got him out the door.

That puncher knew more history
Of the insect race from A to Z
Than any Boston high-brow
Who held an L.F.D.

So discoursin' on their merits
En to give him time to think,
He'd come out with a suggestion
That all hands take a drink.

Besides the three cars loaded,
We had 'bout a half-car more,
So I dumped Tom among the cattle
En shut the stock-car door.

So him en the jug of whiskey
Pulled out on the branch;
I never thought no more about him
Till I got back to the ranch.

Old Andy showed me a telegram
From the firm in K.C. —
The cattle had arrived all safely,
As fine as they could be;

Included in the shipment
Was a cowboy called Tom L. —
Said he was a fightin' cow-puncher,
En his middle name was Hell;

He wanted a return ticket
Back on the line,
Or he'd lick the whole Block outfit,
One at a time!

TOP HAND

*From Jim Brownfield, Crow Flat, New Mexico, winter
of 1899. Authorship credited to Frank Rooney; written
about 1877. This song has been expurgated by me, as
all the old-timers know that as originally sung around the
cow-camps it could not have been printed, as it would
have burned up the paper on which it was written. Jim,
do you remember how you had to force those fresh eggs
down and the jug said, "Goo-Goo"? I published this
song under the title of "Top Hand" in my earlier edition.
The old name, which all cow-punchers remember, did
not sound good in print.*

While you're all so frisky, I'll sing a little song:
Think a horn of whiskey will help the thing along,
It's all about the Top Hand when he's busted flat,
Bumming round town, in his Mexicana hat.
He'd laid up all winter and his pocket-book is flat.
His clothes are all tatters, but he don't mind that.

See him in town with a crowd that he knows
Rolling cigarettes an' a-smoking through his nose.
First thing he tells you, he owns a certain brand,
Leads you to think he is a daisy hand.

Next thing he tells you 'bout his trip up the
     trail,
All the way up to Kansas to finish up his tale.

Put him on a horse, he's a dandy hand to work;
Put him in the branding-pen, he's dead sure to
     shirk.
With natural-leaf tobacco in the pockets of his
     vest
He'll tell you his Californy pants are the best.
He's handled lots of cattle, has n't any fears,
Can draw his sixty dollars, for the balance of his
     years.

Put him on herd, he's a-cussin' all day;
Anything tries, it's sure to get away.
When you have round-up he tells it all about
He's going to do the cuttin' and you can't keep
     him out.
If anything goes wrong he lays it on the screws,
Says the lazy devils were trying to take a snooze.

When he meets a greener he ain't afraid to rig,
Stands him on a chuck-box and makes him dance
     a jig,
Waives a loaded cutter, makes him sing and
     shout,
He's a regular Ben Thompson, when the boss ain't
     about.
When the boss ain't about he leaves his leggins in
     camp,
He swears a man who wears them is worse than a
     tramp.

Says he's not caring for wages that he earns,
For dad's rich in Texas 'n' got wagonloads to
    burn;
But when he goes to town he's sure to take
    it in;
He's always been dreaded wherever he has been.
He rides a fancy horse, he is a favorite man,
Can get more credit than a common waddie can.

When you ship the cattle he's bound to go along
To keep the boss from drinking and to see that
    nothing's wrong;
Wherever he goes, catch on to his game,
He likes to be called with a handle to his name;
He's always primping with a pocket looking-glass;
From the top to the bottom he's a holy jackass.

THE U S U RANGE

*Received this song from Clabe Merchant, Black River,
New Mexico.*

Come, cowboys, and listen to my song;
I'm in hopes I'll please you and not keep you long;
I'll sing you of things you may think strange
About West Texas and the U S U range.

You may go to Stamford and there see a man
Who wears a white shirt and is asking for hands;
You may ask him for work and he'll answer you
    short;
He will hurry you up, for he wants you to start.
He will put you in a wagon and be off in the rain,
You will go upon Tongue River on the U S U range.

You will drive up to the ranch and there you will
       stop;
It's a little sod house with dirt all on top.
You will ask what it is and they will tell you out
       plain
That it is the ranch house on the U S U range.

You will go in the house and he will begin to ex-
       plain;
You will see some blankets rolled up on the floor;
You may ask what it is and they will tell you out
       plain
That it is the bedding on the U S U range.

You are up in the morning at the daybreak
To eat cold beef and U S U steak,
And out to your work no matter if it's rain —
And that is the life on the U S U range.

You work hard all day and come in at night,
And turn your horse loose, for they say it's all right,
And set down to supper and begin to complain
Of the chuck that you eat on the U S U range.

The grub that you get is beans and cold rice
And U S U steak cooked up very nice;
And if you don't like that, you need n't complain,
For that's what you get on the U S U range.

Now, kind friends, I must leave you, I no longer
       can remain,
I hope I have pleased you and given you no pain.
But when I am gone don't think me strange,
For I have been a cow-puncher on the U S U.

WESTERN LIFE

Appeared in "Denver Republican." Accredited to Bronco Sue, who I was told wrote it.

I buckled on a brace of guns and sallied to Wy-
    oming,
And thought I'd kill some Indians ere day had
    reached the gloaming;
But the first red-skin that came to view upon the
    reservation
Said: "Ah, my dear old college chum, I give you
    salutation!"

For Western life ain't wild and woolly now;
They are up on Wagner, Ibsen,
And adore the girls of Gibson —
For Western life ain't wild and woolly now!

I struck a little prairie town and saw two cowboys
    greet,
And thought: "Now there'll be powder burnt when
    these two bad men meet";
But the first one says to Number Two: "You beat
    me, Dick, at tennis:
Now come along, old chap, and read the finish of
    'Pendennis.'"

For Western life ain't wild and woolly now;
The cowboy knows a lot besides more cow;
He can two-step, do hemstitching,
And do hay or baseball pitching —
For Western life ain't wild and woolly now!

So in despair I turned into a busy Western town,
And hoped to see the gun-fighters a-mowing of men
  down;
But while I loitered on the street to see blood by
  the flagon,
I fell before a green-goods man and then a devil
  wagon.

For Western life ain't wild and woolly now;
There is no daily gunpowder powwow;
There are bunco games galore
And the chauffeur holds the floor —
But Western life ain't wild and woolly now!

WESTWARD HO!

*Heard a horse-wrangler named Singleton sing this on the
Delaware, at point of the Guadalupe Mountains.*

I love not Colorado
Where the faro table grows,
And down the desperado
The rippling Bourbon flows;

Nor seek I fair Montana
Of bowie-lunging fame;
The pistol ring of fair Wyoming
I leave to nobler game.

Sweet poker haunted Kansas
In vain allures the eye;
The Nevada rough has charms enough,
Yet its blandishments I fly.

Shall Arizona woo me
Where the meek Apache hides?
Or New Mexico where natives grow
With arrow-proof insides?

Nay, 'tis where the grizzlies wander
And the lonely diggers roam,
And the grim Chinese from the squatter flees,
That I'll make my humble home.

I'll chase the wild tarantula
And the fierce coyote I'll dare,
And the locust grim, I'll battle him.
In his native wildwood lair.

Or I'll seek the gulch deserted,
And dream of the wild red man,
And I'll build a cot on a corner lot
And get rich as soon as I can.

WHAT'S BECOME OF THE PUNCHERS?

By N. Howard Thorp

What's become of the punchers
We rode with long ago?
The hundreds and hundreds of cowboys
We all of us used to know?

Sure, some were killed by lightning,
Some when the cattle run,
Others were killed by horses,
And some with the old six-gun.

Those that worked on the round-up,
Those of the branding-pen,
Those who went out on the long trail drive
And never returned again.

We know of some who have prospered,
We hear of some who are broke,
My old pardner made millions in Tampa,
While I've got my saddle in soak!

Sleeping and working together,
Eatin' old " Cussie's good chuck,"
Riding in all kinds of weather,
Playing in all kinds of luck;

Bragging about our top-hosses,
Each puncher ready to bet
His horse could outrun the boss's,
Or any old horse you could get!

Scott lies in Tularosa,
Elmer Price lies near Santa Fe,
While Randolph sits here by the fireside
With a " flat-face " on his knee.

'Gene Rhodes is among the high-brows,
A-writin' up the West,
But I know a lot of doin's
That he never has confessed!

He used to ride 'em keerless
In the good old days
When we both worked together
In the San Andres!

Building big loops we called "blockers,"
Spinning the rope in the air,
Never a cent in our pockets,
But what did a cow-puncher care?

I'm tired of riding this trail, boys,
Dead tired of riding alone —
B'lieve I'll head old Button for Texas,
Towards my old Palo Pinto home!

WHEN BOB GOT THROWED

Author unknown. Heard it sung in Arizona at Hachita by a puncher named Livingston.

That time when Bob got throwed
I thought I sure would bust;
I liked to died a-laffin'
To see him chewing dust.

He crawled on that pinto bronc
And hit him with a quirt,
The next thing that he knew
He was wallerin' in the dirt.

Yes, it might 'a' killed him,
I heard the hard ground pop,
But to see if he was injured
You bet I didn't stop.

I jest rolled on the ground
And began to kick and yell;
It liked to tickled me to death
To see how hard he fell.

'T war n't more than a week ago
That I myself got throwed;
But that was from a meaner horse
Than old Bob ever rode.

D' you reckon Bob looked sad and said
"I hope that you ain't hurt"?
Naw; he just laughed and laughed
To see me chewin' dirt.

I've been prayin' ever since
For his horse to turn his pack,
And when he done it I'd 'a' laughed
If it had broke his back.

So I was still a-howlin'
When Bob he got up lame;
He seen his horse had run clear off,
And so for me he came.

He first chucked sand into my eyes,
With a rock he rubbed my head,
Then he twisted both my arms:
"Now, go fetch that hoss," he said.

So I went and fetched him back,
But I was feelin' good all day;
For I sure enough do love to see
A fellow get throwed that way.

WHOSE OLD COW?

By N. Howard Thorp

Written at Roswell, New Mexico, 1899. Add was one of the best cow-hands on Pecos River. Everybody knew him. When he got married each cow-man wanted to give him a present, no one knowing what the other man had sent him, " as ranches were far apart." He received nineteen stoves and ranges for wedding presents. This song was in my copyrighted book published in 1908.

'T was the end of the round-up the last day of
     June,
Or maybe July, I don't just remember,
Or it might have been August, 't was sometime
     ago,
Or perhaps 't was the first of September.

Anyhow, 't was the round-up we had at Mayou,
On the lightning rod's range near Cayo;
There was some twenty wagons " more or less "
     camped about
On the temporal in the cañon.

First night we'd no cattle, so we only stood guard
On the horses, somewhere about two hundred head;
So we side-lined and hoppled, we belled and we
     staked,
Loosed our hot rolls and fell into bed.

Next morning 'bout daybreak we started our work;
Our horses, like possums, felt fine,
Each one " tendin' kitten," none trying to shirk,
So the round-up got on in good time.

Well, we worked for a week till the country was
    clear
An' the boss said, "Now boys we'll stay here;
We'll carve and we'll trim 'em an' start out a
    herd
Up the east trail from old Abilene."

Next morning all on herd an' but two with the cut,
An' the boss on Piute carving fine,
'Til he rode down his horse and had to pull out,
An' a new man went in to clean up.

Well, after each outfit had worked on the band
There was only three head of them left,
When Nig Add from the L F D outfit rode in,
A dictionary on earmarks an' brands.

He cut the two head out where they belonged,
But when the last cow stood there alone,
Add's eyes bulged so he didn't know just what to
    say,
'Ceptin' "Boss, dere's sumpin' here monstrous
    wrong!

"White folks smarter 'n Add, an' maybe I'se wrong'
But here's six months' wages dar I'll give
If any one 'll tell me when I reads de mark
To who dis long-horned cow belongs.

"Left ear swaller fork an' de undercrop,
Overslope in right ear an' de underbit,
Hole punched in center, an' de jinglebob
Under half crop, an' de slash an' split.

"She's got O Block an' Lightnin' Rod,
Nine Forty-Six an' A Bar Eleven,
Rafter Cross an' de double prod,
Terrapin an' Ninety-Seven;

"Half Circle A an' Diamond D,
Four-Cross L an' Three P Z;
B W I, Bar X V V,
Bar N Cross an' A L C.

"So, if none o' you punchers claims dis cow,
Mr. Stock 'Sociation need n't get 'larmed,
So old nigger Add, just brand her now,
For one more brand or less won't do no harm."

WINDY BILL

*Sung first to me by John Collier, Cornudas Mountain,
New Mexico, July, 1899. Appeared first in my previous
copyrighted book.*

Windy Bill was a Texas man,
  And he could rope, you bet;
Talk of the steer he could n't tie down
  Had n't sorter been born yet;
The boys they knew of an old black steer,
  A sort of an old outlaw,
Who ran down in the bottom
  Just at the foot of the draw.

This slim black steer had stood his ground
  With punchers from everywhere;
The boys they bet Bill two to one
  He could n't quite get there.

So Bill brought up his old cow-horse —
  His wethers and back were sore —
Prepared to tackle this old black steer
  Who ran down in the draw.

With his grazin' bits and sand-stacked tree,
  His chaps and taps to boot,
His old maguey tied hard and fast,
  Went out to tackle the brute.
Bill sorter sauntered around him first;
  The steer began to paw,
Poked up his tail high in the air,
  And lit down in the draw.

The old cow-horse flew at him
  Like he 'd been eatin' corn,
And Bill he landed his old maguey
  Around old blackie's horns.
The old-time horse he stopped dead-still;
  The cinches broke like straw;
Both the sand-stacked tree and old maguey,
  Went driftin' down the draw.

Bill landed in a big rock-pile;
  His hands and face were scratched;
He 'lowed he always could tie a steer
  But guessed he 'd found his match.
Paid up his bet like a little man,
  Without a bit of jaw,
And said old blackie was the boss
  Of all down in the draw.

There 's a moral to my song, boys,
  Which I hope you can see;

Whenever you start to tackle a steer
  Never tie hard your maguey.
Put on your dalebueltas,
  'Cordin' to California law,
And you will never see your old rim-fires
  Driftin' down the draw.

WOMEN OUTLAWS

By N. Howard Thorp

There's a touch of human pathos,
A glamour of the West,
Round the names of women outlaws
Who have now gone to their rest —

Bronco Sue, Belle Star, and Shudders,
Pike Kate, and Altar Doane,
Calamity Jane, Sister Cummings,
And the Rose of Cimmaron.

You've all oft heard the saying,
"I'd go to Hell for you!"
About these women outlaws
That saying was too true.

Each left her home and dear one
For the man she loved the best,
Close by his side on many a wild ride
Through the mountains of the West.

They've played their parts in Western Drama,
On the great unscreened Western stage,
Where the mountains were their platform,
Their stage-setting rocks and sage.

Hunted by many a posse,
Always on the run,
Every man's hand against them,
They fought, and often won.

With a price upon each head,
They'd have to fight and stand,
And die as game as any man
With a gun in either hand.

My hat off to you, women outlaws,
For you did what you thought best,
And the same wild blood that coursed your veins
Has settled up the West.

Whether right or wrong, your spirit
Knew not the word of fear —
And 't is the dauntless courage of your kind
That bred the pioneer!

THE ZEBRA DUN

First heard the song sung by Randolph Reynolds, Carrizozo Flats, in 1890.

We were camped on the plains at the head of
    the Cimarron
When along came a stranger and stopped to arger
    some.
He looked so very foolish that we began to look
    around,
We thought he was a greenhorn that had just
    'scaped from town.

We asked if he had been to breakfast; he had n't
    had a smear;
So we opened up the chuck-box and bade him have
    his share.
He took a cup of coffee and some biscuits and some
    beans,
And then began to talk and tell about foreign kings
    and queens, —

About the Spanish War and fighting on the seas
With guns as big as steers and ramrods big as
    trees, —
And about old Paul Jones, a mean-fighting son of a
    gun,
Who was the grittiest cuss that ever pulled a gun.

Such an educated feller, his thoughts just came in
    herds,
He astonished all them cowboys with them jaw-
    breaking words.
He just kept on talking till he made the boys all sick,
And they began to look around just how to play
    a trick.

He said he had lost his job upon the Santa Fe
And was going across the plains to strike the 7-D.
He did n't say how come it, some trouble with the
    boss,
But said he 'd like to borrow a nice fat saddle hoss.

This tickled all the boys to death; they laughed 'way
    down in their sleeves, —
" We will lend you a horse just as fresh and fat as
    you please."

Shorty grabbed a lariat and roped the Zebra Dun
And turned him over to the stranger and waited
for the fun.

Old Dunny was a rocky outlaw that had grown so
awful wild
That he could paw the white out of the moon
every jump for a mile.
Old Dunny stood right still — as if he didn't
know —
Until he was saddled and ready for to go.

When the stranger hit the saddle, Old Dunny quit
the earth,
And traveled right straight up for all that he was
worth.
A-pitching and a-squealing, a-having wall-eyed
fits,
His hind feet perpendicular, his front ones in the
bits.

We could see the tops of the mountains under
Dunny every jump,
But the stranger he was growed there just like
the camel's hump;
The stranger sat upon him and curled his black
mustache,
Just like a summer boarder waiting for his hash.

He thumped him in the shoulders and spurred
him when he whirled,
To show them flunky punchers that he was the wolf
of the world.

When the stranger had dismounted once more upon
the ground,
We knew he was a thoroughbred and not a gent
from town;

The boss, who was standing round watching of the
show,
Walked right up to the stranger and told him he
need n't go, —
"If you can use the lasso like you rode old Zebra
Dun,
You are the man I 've been looking for ever since
the year one."

Oh, he could twirl the lariat, and he did n't do it
slow;
He could catch them fore feet nine out of ten for
any kind of dough.
There 's one thing and a shore thing I 've learned
since I 've been born,
That every educated feller ain't a plumb greenhorn.

GLOSSARY

GLOSSARY

Baquero (vaquero)	A cowpuncher
Blocker	A large loop made with a rope
Bronco	An untamed horse
Broom'y, broom tails	Range mares
Buckaroo	A cowpuncher
Caballada	A bunch of horses
Cabresto	A rope
Chaps, chaparreras	Leather leggins
Cincha	A girth for saddle
Corral	A pen or enclosure
Crinolina	Hoop-skirt. An expression used to describe spinning a rope
Cuarta	A whip
Dale vuelta	Used in giving turns of rope around saddle horn
Freno	A bridle
Grazin bits	A snaffle or easy curb
Jáquima	A halter
Kack	A saddle
Lasso	A loop, or to catch
Latigo	A strap from cinch to saddle
Maguey	A Mexican catch rope
Manada	A bunch of mares
Maverick	An unbranded animal
Mesteño	A wild horse
Montura	A saddle
Morral	A feed bag
Mustang	A wild horse
Outlaw	A horse which has been spoiled in breaking

Reata	A rope
Remuda	A bunch of saddle horses or relay of horses
Rodéo	A round-up
Slick	An unbranded calf
Taps, tapaderas	Stirrup coverings
Tarp	A canvas bed sheet
Vaquero	A cowpuncher
Waddie	A cowpuncher
Willows	Range mares
Wrangler	A man who looks after and outfits saddle horses

INDEX OF FIRST LINES

INDEX OF FIRST LINES